OPTIONS TRADING: CRASH COURSE

Master The Options Game With This Ultimate Guide To Investing. Dominate Advanced Strategies, Make Money, Create Cashflow With Passive Income And Get Your Financial Freedom

MARK KRATTER

Table of Contents

Introduction

Having financial freedom is more than just having a 6-month emergency fund saved up and your debt cleared. Financial freedom means taking control of your time and finances so that you can do the things that you want to do rather than what your bank account figure dictates. Being financially free means you do not need to trade your time for money.

To be able to gain this financial freedom, you need to have financial security. Financial security is the condition whereby you support the standard of living you want now and in the future by having stable sources of income and other resources available to you. That means not living paycheck to paycheck. It means not having to worry about where your next dollar will come from. It means having a huge weight lifted off your shoulders because you know there are resources that you can leverage to get the things that you want and need.

People who have financial freedom are also financially independent. Financial independence is the state of having personal wealth to maintain the lifestyle and the standard of living you want without actually having to trade your daily hours for money. The assets and resources that you have generated will gain that income for you so that your income remains far greater than your expenses. In essence, being financially independent means that you can go for a prolonged period of time without trading time for money and still have the standard of living that you want. That you can go on a year-long vacation and still be secure in the knowledge that your wealth is still growing.

To be financially independent, you have to have:

An emergency fund that can sustain your lifestyle for an extended period of time (years).

Assets that produce income for you on a daily, weekly, monthly and yearly basis.

Very little or zero debt.

Very few people on the planet are financially secure and independent. In fact, more than 1 billion people live in extreme poverty. In 2015, it was estimated that more than 10% of the global population lived on less than US$1.90 per day.

Despite these statistics, there is hope. This hope comes from the fact that this statistic goes down every year. In fact, in 2019 less than 8% of the global population lived in extreme poverty. This is largely attributed to the fact that people being more educated about their options and are not just accepting of these poor circumstances.

Despite this improvement, most of the global population still trades their time for an hourly wage. The income earned from this is not sustainable nor will it allow them to live the standard of life that they would like. They will not be able to retire comfortably. There is no power or security in living this way.

People who are financially free have learned and harnessed the power of passive income. Passive income is wealth that is generated from little to no effort or earned in the way of exchanging time for money over the long term. While it might take a massive amount of time and effort to establish in the beginning, passive income allows you to earn money even while you sleep with little to no daily effort required for its maintenance.

The beauty of passive income is that it is not only limited to one income bracket or portion of the population. Anyone can develop passive income as long as they develop the right mindset and is willing to put in the time and effort to learn and be consistent in pursuing this standard of living.

CHAPTER 1:

Options Trading Basics

What Are Stock Options

To get an understanding of the meaning of stock options, we first have to know the meaning of the two words independently.

Stock refers to:

- The total money a company has from selling shares to individuals.

- A portion of the ownership of the company that can be sold to members of the public

Option (finance) refers to:

A contract that provides the buyer with the right, though not the obligation, to sell or buy an asset at an agreed-upon strike price at a specified date based on the type of option

Now that we know the meaning of both stocks and options, we can easily define stock options. We can define the term in the following ways:

Stock options provide an investor with the right to sell or buy a stock at a set price and date.

The stock option can also refer to an advantage in the form of an opportunity provided by a company to any employee to buy shares in a company at an agreed-upon fixed price or a discount.

Stock options have been a topic of interest in recent years. We are having more and more people engaging in options trading. The profitability of stock options has resulted in a lot of debates. Some say it's a scam; others claim that it is not a worthy investment while others say that they are minting millions from it. All these speculations draw us to one question, which is what are stock options? For us to accurately answer this question, we will have to go through stock options keenly. We will be required to know all about it and what it entails. This information makes it easy to make judgments with actual facts as opposed to using assumptions. You will get to say something that you can actually back up. Having knowledge gives you an added advantage and places you in a powerful position.

Understanding Stock Options

For us to understand stock options, we consider the following:

Strike Price

For one to know if a stock can be exercised, they will need to consider the strike price. By the time an option gets to the expiration date, there is a price that it is expected to have. This price should be lower or higher than the stock price, and it is what we refer to as the strike price of an underlying asset. If as an investor, you predict that the value of the stock will increase, you can purchase a call option at the set strike price.

When it comes to putting options, the strike price will be the price at which an asset is traded by the option buyer by the time the contract expires. The strike price can also be referred to as the exercise price. It is a major factor to consider while establishing the option value. Depending on when the options are carried out, the strike price will differ. As an investor, it is good to keep track of the strike price since it helps in identifying the quality of an investment.

Styles

There are two main option styles. These are European and American options styles. If you intend to engage in options trading, it is advisable to equip yourself with knowledge of the various styles. As you analyze the styles, you will identify those that work for you and those that do not. You will also find that some styles are easier to learn and handle as opposed to others. You can decide to engage in the one that is convenient for you and avoid engaging in the style that you have difficulties understanding. The American style option allows one to exercise a trade any period between the time of purchase and the time a contract expires. Most traders engage in this style due to its convenience. It allows one to carry out a trade any period within which a contract is considered to be valid. The European style option is not commonly used as compared to the American style. In the European option style, a trader can only exercise their options during the expiration date. If you are not an expert in options trading, I would advise you to avoid using the European style.

Expiration date

An expiration date refers to the period in which a contract is regarded as worthless. Stocks have expiration dates. The period between when they were purchased and the expiry date, indicate the validity of an option. As a trader, you are expected to utilize the contracts to your advantage, within this time frame. You can trade as much as you can and get high returns within the period of buying and the period of expiry. Learn to utilize the time provided adequately. If you are not careful, the option may expire before you get a chance to exercise it. We have may beginners who assume this factor and end up making heavy losses. You will be required to be keen while engaging in the stock market. Forgetting to look into the expiry date may result in your stocks being regarded as worthless without getting a chance of investing in them. In some rare cases, the stocks are exercised during the expiry date. This is common in the European option. I would not encourage a beginner to engage in this type of option. It is tricky and could lead to a loss if you are not careful while carrying out the trade.

Contacts

Contracts refer to the amount of shares an investor is intending to purchase. One hundred shares of an underlying asset are equal to one contract. Contracts aid in establishing the value of s stock. Contracts tend to be valuable before the expiry date. After the expiry date, a contract can be regarded as worthless. Knowing this will help you discover the best time to exercise a contract. In a case where a trader purchases ten contracts, he or she gets to 10 $ 350 calls. When the stock prices go above $ 350, at the expiry trade, the trader gets the chance to buy or sell 1000 shares of their stock at $350. This happens regardless of the stock price at that particular time. In an event whereby the stock is lower than $350, the option will expire worthlessly. This will result in making a complete loss as an investor. You will lose the whole amount you used to purchase options, and there is no way of getting it back. If you intend to invest in options trading, it is good to become aware of the contracts and how you can exercise them for a profitable options trading outcome.

Premium

The premium refers to the money used to purchase options. You can obtain the premium by multiplying the call price and the number of contracts by 100. The '100' is the number of shares per contract. This is more like the investment made by the trader expecting great returns. While investing, you will expect that the investment you chose to engage in will result in a profitable outcome. No one gets in business anticipating a loss. You find that one is always hopeful that the investment they have chosen to engage in will be beneficial. You will constantly look forward to getting the best out of a trade.

The above factors tell us more about stocks. In case you were stuck and didn't fully understand what stocks entail, now you have a better understanding. You will come across numerous terms when you decide to engage in stocks. Do not let the terms scare you; they are mostly things you knew, but just didn't know that they go by those terms. We have many people who are quite investing in stocks, just because they could not understand the various terms being used. This should not be the case. You can take some time to go through the terms and understand what they entail carefully.

Options in Stock Market

Stock options are not as hard as people make them appear. At times people try to make them seem difficult, yet it is an easy thing that can be grasped by almost everyone. As a beginner, do not be discouraged into thinking that options trading is a difficult investment. You will be surprised how easy it is, and you will wonder why you never invested in it sooner. When engaging in stock options, there are four factors the investors will have to consider. Putting these factors into consideration will have a positive impact on their trade.

The Right, But Not the Obligation

What comes in your mind when you read this statement? Well, when we talk or rights, we mean that you have the freedom to purchase a certain type of option. When we talk of obligation, we are referring to the fact that one does not have a legal authority to exercise a duty. Options do not give traders a legal authority to carry out a duty. This means that there is freedom to trade, but it is not legally mandated.

Buying or Selling

As a trader, you are given the right to purchase or trade an option. There are two types of stock that one can choose from. We have the put option and the call option. Both differ and have their individual pros and cons. If you intend trading in options, it is important that you equip yourself with adequate knowledge before trading or purchasing stocks. This information will have an impact on your expected income. The stocks you choose to buy or sell will dictate if you will earn high returns or if you will end up making a loss.

Set Price

There is a certain price that has been set to exercise the option. The price will vary depending on the option type. Some stock options tend to be valued more than other options. There are a number of factors that will influence the price of options.

Expiry Date

The expiry date is when a contract will be considered useless. Stock options have an expiry date. The date is set to determine the value of an option. Any period before the expiration date, a contact is regarded as being valid. This means that it can be utilized to generate income at any point before the expiry date. When it gets to the expiry date, a trader has no power to exercise the option. This is as a result of the contract being regarded as worthless. As an investor, it is good to constantly ensure that your investment is within the duration of its validity.

CHAPTER 2:

Strategies for Beginners

I have to admit it -- I'm a covered calls junkie.

I've been selling covered calls since 1996 and have made hundreds of thousands of dollars in the process.

After all these years, I'm still amazed that someone is willing to pay me for the chance to take my stock off my hands for a profit.

There is a common misconception that trading options is inherently riskier than trading stocks. It's easy to see where this misconception comes from: many people do indeed trade options in a reckless manner. Options can be used to magnify returns on the upside, and the downside. In inexperienced or greedy hands, this can be a recipe for disaster.

Most of these reckless traders are buying options. The strategy that you are about to learn involves selling options.

Here's how it works:

You buy a stock, and then enter into a contract ("you sell some call options"). This contract says that you will get paid some cash today (the "premium"), in exchange for giving up the stock's potential upside past a certain point. Maybe you buy 100 shares of stock XYZ at 20.00 and agree to give up all potential upside past 21.00 ("the strike price"). In exchange, you get paid $1.00 per share (or $100, since you own 100 shares).

Let's review what just happened: you bought a stock at 20.00 and immediately got paid 1.00. In effect, you have only paid 19.00 for the stock.

If the stock goes to zero the next day, you lose 19.00 (or $1,900 since you own 100 shares). On the other hand, if you had bought the stock without entering into the contract, and the stock went to zero the next day, you would have lost 20.00 (or $2,000 since you own 100 shares).

Hopefully this shows how covered calls can actually decrease the risk of a long stock position.

So, what are the risks associated with covered calls?

Risk #1: Lost upside

Risk #2: See risk #1

The riskiest thing about covered calls is that you miss out on a stock's appreciation past a certain point.

If you sold covered calls on Apple (AAPL) back when it was $100 (pre-split) and then it ran up past $800, you left a pretty big chunk of change on the table.

But what if instead you held General Electric (GE) in your account over the past 2 years? (I'm writing this in May 2015.) You have watched the stock bounce between 23 and 28, pretty much going nowhere.

You've been paid a small dividend while you waited but have otherwise been treading water. In this case, selling covered calls on the position would have generated significantly higher returns.

The moral?

Don't apply the covered calls strategy to stocks that you think will appreciate sharply in the near future.

Covered calls work best on stocks that are trading sideways, or slightly up.

If you own a stock in your long-term portfolio, and you don't think it is going anywhere over the short term, covered calls are an excellent strategy to generate some monthly income while you wait.

A Step-by-Step Guide to Selling Covered Calls
back to top

First, let's go over some basic terminology.

A "call option" (or just a "call") is a contract that gives you the right to buy a stock at a certain price, over a certain period of time, until the option expires. If you own a call option ("are long a call"), you have the right to buy the stock, but you don't have to buy the stock.

So, for example, let's look at a KO June 41.00 call.

"KO" is simply the ticker of the underlying stock, in this case, Coke ("The Coca-Cola Company").

"June" is what is called the option's "expiration date." This is the month when the options contract expires.

Expiration usually occurs at the end of the day on the 3rd Friday of the month, or 19 June 2015 in this case.

"41.00" is the "strike price": this is the price at which the owner of the call option has the right to purchase the stock (or "call it away" from its owner, hence the name "call").

If you buy a call ("if you are long a call"), you are betting that the stock will move up in price.

If you sell a call ("if you are short a call"), you are betting that the stock will stay roughly where it is or move down in price.

If you sell a call, and the underlying stock moves up a lot in price, you can lose a lot of money, and end up having to buy back the call at a higher price. If you are just short a call, it is called a "naked call." It is a naked call because you are "exposed" to sharp up moves in the stock.

Covered calls are much safer.

When trading covered calls, we buy a stock and then sell an equivalent amount of call options at a strike price that is just above where we bought the stock. If the stock moves up sharply, you will lose money on the short call position, but you will make back an equal amount on the long stock position. In other words, you are "covered" and don't have the huge risk of loss that you do with naked calls.

There are times when it can be advantageous to sell naked calls, but that is an advanced strategy, and the subject for another book.

For now, you should stick to covered calls.

Let's look at a real example to make this clear.

As I'm writing this, Coke (KO) is trading at $40.94 per share.

I like Coke at this price, and so I decide to sell covered calls on it.

To make the numbers easy, let's assume that I have enough money to buy 1,000 shares of Coke.

If you are trading a small account ($5,000 or less), there is a special way of doing covered calls that you can learn about here:

So, if I have the capital, I buy 1,000 shares at 40.94. This costs me $40,940, plus a $4.95 commission (if you're using TradeKing), for a grand total of $40,944.95.

Now I immediately decide to sell calls against this stock position.

To get an options quote, I navigate to Yahoo Finance, enter the symbol KO, then click on "Options" in the left-hand menu.

This link should take you there:

http://finance.yahoo.com/q/op?s=KO+Options

Next, I go to the drop-down menu for the date, and select June 12, 2015, which is about 30 days from today.

I choose the strike price that is just above my purchase price: this strike price is 41.00.

I've already chosen an expiration date from the drop-down: June 12, 2015. This is the date that the contract ends ("expires").

Here's what it looks like on Yahoo Finance today. If you'd like to expand the image, just double-click on it:

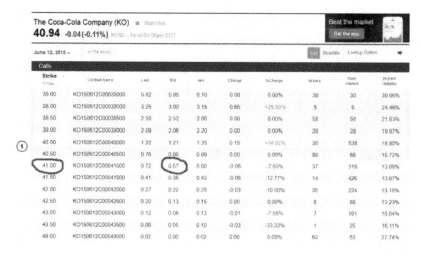

I've circled the strike price ("41") as well as the bid price ("0.57"). The bid is the price that the market is willing to pay for a call option. Since I am selling calls, I should set my limit order to the bid price, if I would like my order to be filled right away.

Each call option covers 100 shares of stock. So, if I now own 1,000 shares of Coke, I need to sell 10 (1,000 divided by 100) call options.

So, I sell 10 call options to the bid (use the order type "sell to open"), and my order is filled. If I used TradeKing.com, I was charged a commission of $4.95 base rate plus 10 contracts times $0.65 per contract, or $11.45. I sold 10 calls, and so my account was credited with 10 calls times 100 shares per call times 0.57 (the price at which I sold the calls), or $570.

My net credit after the commission is $570.00 minus $11.45, or $558.55.

I get to keep this $558.55 ("the premium") no matter what happens.

I am still long the 1,000 shares of Coke that I bought.

And I am "short" 10 call options in my account. I am "short" because I sold something that I didn't have. Don't worry about this for now.

As the price of the stock trades up, the shares of Coke will gain in value, while the short call position loses roughly an equal amount (more on this later).

As the price of the stock trades down, the shares of Coke will lose value, while the short call position will make money.

As we mentioned before, covered calls work best in a flat to slightly up market.

CHAPTER 3:

Pricing and Volatility Strategies

While the stock market has long term trends that investors rely on fairly well as the years and decades go by, over the short term the stock market is highly volatile. By that, we mean that prices are fluctuating up and down and doing so over short time periods. Volatility is something that long-term investors ignore. It's why you will hear people that promote conservative investment strategies suggesting that buyers use dollar cost averaging. What this does is it averages out the volatility in the market. That way you don't risk making the mistake of buying stocks when the price is a bit higher than it should be, because you'll average that out by buying shares when it's a bit lower than it should be.

In a sense, over the short term, the stock market can be considered as a chaotic system. So from one day to the next, unless there is something specific on offer, like Apple introducing a new gadget that investors are going to think will be a major hit, you can't be sure what the stock price is going to be tomorrow or the day after that. An increase on one day doesn't mean more increases are coming; it might be followed by a major dip the following day.

For example, at the time of writing, checking Apple's stock price, on the previous Friday it bottomed out at $196. Over the following days, it went up and down several times, and on the most recent close, it was $203. The movements over a short-term period appear random, and to a certain extent, they are. It's only over the long term that we see the actual direction that Apple is heading.

Of course, Apple is at the end of a ten-year run that began with the introduction of the iPhone and iPad. It's a reasonable bet that while it's a solid long-term investment, the stock probably isn't going to be moving enough for the purposes of making good profits over the short term from trades on call options (not to mention the per share price is relatively high).

The truth is volatility is actually a friend of the trader who buys call options. But it's a friend you have to be wary of because you can benefit from volatility while also getting in big trouble from it.

The reason stocks with more volatility are the friend of the options trader is that in part the options trader is playing a probability game. In other words, you're looking for stocks that have a chance of beating the strike price you need in order to make profits. A volatile stock that has large movements has a greater probability of not only passing your strike price but doing so in such a fashion that it far exceeds your strike price enabling you to make a large profit.

Of course, the alternative problem exists – that the stock price will suddenly drop. That is why care needs to be a part of your trader's toolkit. A stock with a high level of volatility is just as likely to suddenly drop in price as it is to skip right past your strike price.

Moreover, while you're a beginner and might get caught with your pants down, volatile stocks are going to attract experienced options traders. That means that the stock will be in high demand when it comes to options contracts. What happens when there is a high demand for something? The price shoots up. In the case of call options, that means the stock will come with a higher premium. You will need to take the higher premium into account when being able to exercise your options at the right time and make sure the price is high enough above your strike price that you don't end up losing money.

Traders take some time to examine the volatility of a given stock over the recent past, but they also look into what's known as implied volatility. This is a kind of weather forecast for stocks. It's an estimate of the future price movements of a stock, and it has a large influence on the pricing of options. Implied volatility is denoted by the Greek symbol σ, implied volatility increases in bear markets, and it actually decreases when investors are bullish. Implied volatility is a tool that can provide insight into the options future value.

For options traders, more volatility is a good thing. A stock that doesn't have much volatility is going to be a stable stock whose price isn't going to change very much over the lifetime of a contract. So while you may want to sell a covered call for a stock with low volatility, you're probably not going to want to buy one if you're buying call options because that means there will be a lower probability that the stock will change enough to exceed the strike price so you can earn a profit on a trade. Remember too that stocks that are very volatile will attract a lot of interest from options traders and command higher premiums. You will have to do some balancing in picking stocks that are of interest.

Being able to pick stocks that will have the right amount of volatility so that you can be sure of getting one that will earn profits on short term trades is something you're only going to get from experience. You should spend some time practicing before actually investing large amounts of money. That is, pick stocks you are interested in and make your bets but don't actually make the trades. Then follow them over the time period of the contract and see what happens. In the meantime, you can purchase safer call options, and so using this two-pronged approach gain experience that will lead to more surefire success down the road.

One thing that volatility means for everyone is that predicting the future is an impossible exercise. You're going to have some misses no matter how much knowledge and experience you gain. The only thing to aim for is to beat the market more often than you lose. The biggest mistake you can make is putting your life savings into a single stock that you think is a sure thing and then losing it all.

Options to pursue if your options aren't working

At this point, you may think that if the underlying stock for your option doesn't go anywhere or it tanks that you have no choice but to wait out the expiration date and count the money you spend on your premiums as a loss. That really isn't the case. The truth is you can sell a call option you've purchased to other traders in the event it's not working for you. Of course, you're not going to make a profit taking this approach in the vast majority of cases. But it will give you a chance to recoup some of your losses. If you have invested in a large number of call options for a specific stock and it's causing you problems, you need to recoup at least some of your losses may be more acute. Of course, the right course of action in these cases is rarely certain, especially if the expiration date for the contract is relatively far off in the future, which could mean that the stock has many chances to turn around and beat your strike price. Remember, in all bad scenarios actually buying the shares of stock is an option – you're not required to do it. In all cases, the biggest loss you're facing is losing the entire premium. You'll also want to keep the following rule of thumb in mind at all times – the more time value an option has, the higher the price you can sell the option for. If there isn't much time value left, then you're probably going to have to sell the option at a discount. If there is a lot of time value, you may be able to recoup most of your losses on the premium.

CHAPTER 4:

Calls and Puts Options

Put and call options are referred to as a derivative investment. The movements of their prices depend on the movements of prices of a different financial product, also referred to as the underlying.

So, what is an option? It is defined as the right to sell or buy a certain stock with a set price given a specific time frame. With options, you won't have outright ownership of the shares, but you make calculated bets on a stock's price and what its value will be in the future, given the specified expiration of the option. What makes options attractive is that you are to choose whether you want to exercise them or not. If your bet is wrong, you can let the options expire. Although the options' original cost is lost, it still wouldn't compare had you paid for the stock's full price.

Call options are purchased when the trader is expecting the underlying's price to go up within a particular time frame.

Put options are purchased when the trader is expecting the underlying's price to go down within a particular time frame.

There's an option for puts and calls to be written or sold. This will still generate income, but certain rights have to be given up to the option's buyer.

For options defined for the US, a call is defined as an options contract giving the buyer rights to buy an underlying asset at a previously set price any time until the expiration date. For options defined for the EU, buyers can choose to exercise the option to purchase the underlying but only on the set expiration date.

The strike price is defined as a price previously determined at which the call buyer has the choice to purchase the underlying asset. For example, a buyer of a certain stock call option with a 10$ strike price may opt to purchase that stock at the same price before the expiration date of the option.

The expiration of options may vary. It can also be short or long term. It can be worth the while for call buyers to exercise the option, which is to require the writer or seller of the call to sell the stocks at the set strike price., but only if the underlying's current price is more than the strike price. For example, if a stock trades at $10 at the stock market, it is not profitable for the buyer of the call option to exercise the choice to purchase that stock at $11 since they could get the same on the market at a lower price.

Put buyers reserve the right to sell stocks at strike price during a set time range.

The highs and lows the stock market goes through can be both exciting and nerve-wracking for newbie or veteran investors. Risking hard-earned money can make anyone anxious. But played right with sound and well-planned strategies, you can be successful in this field

If you are looking for a way to invest in the stock market but you are trying to avoid the risk of directly selling stocks or buying them, options trading might be perfect for you. Options are typically traded at significantly lower prices compared to the underlying prices of the actual shares. This makes trading them a less risky way to control a large stock position, although you don't own the shares. Using options strategically allows risk mitigation while maintaining huge profit potentials, and you will be playing in the field even if you're investing just a fraction of the stock's price.

All of these benefits of options trading got you excited, right? After all, options have a lower risk and they're a lot cheaper. There are two major disadvantages, however – the limited-time aspect and the reality that you don't own the stock until you choose to exercise your options.

Call Options

With call options, what you pay for is just 'rights to buy' certain shares at a set price and covered by a specific time frame. Let's say that stock ABC is selling for $90 per share in May. If you believe that the stock's price will go up over a few months, you'd purchase a three-month option to buy 100 shares of ABC by August 31 for $100. For this sample call option, you would be paying around $200 if the option cost per share is $2. In options, you are only allowed to buy in increments of 100 shares. This gives you the choice to purchase 100 shares of ABC anytime within the three-month timeframe. The $200 investment is significantly lower than the $9,000 you would have had to shell out if you bought 1000 shares outright.

If you bet right and on July 15, if the ABC shares hit the market at $115, you may exercise the call option and you would have gained $1,300 (that's 100 shares multiplied by the $15 profit you gained per share and deducted by your original investment of $200). If you don't have the resources to buy the shares, you can also make a profit if you re-sell the option to another investor or via the open market. The gain will be pretty much similar to this option.

If you bet wrong, and the price of ABC's shares fell to $80 never to reach $100 within the three-month timeframe, you can let the option reach its expiration, which saves you money (if you bought the shares outright, your original investment of $9,000 is now down to a value of only $8,000, so you lost $1000). This means you only lost $200, which was your investment for the call option.

Risks Involved in Call Options

Like any other form of investment, options have their share of potential risks. Taking the second scenario where you bet wrong as an example and stock ABC never got to $100 during the option's timeframe of three months, you would have lost the entire $200 of your investment, right? In terms of loss percentage, that's %100. Anyone who's been playing the stock market would tell you that it's extremely rare for an investor to suffer a 100% loss. This scenario can only happen if ABC suddenly went bankrupt, causing the price of their stocks to plummet down to zero value.

Therefore, if you look at it from a point of view of percentages, options can cause you huge losses. Let's elaborate on this point. If the price of ABC's share went up to $99 and it's the last day for you to exercise the option, choosing to purchase the shares will mean losing a dollar for each share. What if you invested $9,000 for the stock and you owned 100 stock shares? In three months, which is the option's expiration date if you took it, you would have gained 10% from your original investment ($99 from $90). Comparing both, you would have gained 10% if you purchased the shares outright and lost %100 if you chose the option but did not exercise it. This example shows how risky options can be.

However, the opposite can happen if stock ABC reached a price higher than $100. If you purchased the option, your gain percentage would have been substantially higher compared to buying the stocks outright. If the stock reached $110, you would have gained 400% ($10 gain versus the $2 per share investment) if you went for the option and only gained 22% ($20 gain versus the $90 per share investment) if you purchased the shares.

Lastly, when you own the stock, nothing can force you to sell. That means if after three months, and stock ABC's price goes down, you can hang on to it if you believe it still has the potential to recover and even increase in value compared to the original. If the price goes up dramatically, you'll make significant gains and you didn't incur losses. However, if you chose options as your investment method, the expiration would have forced you to suffer a 100% loss after the set timeframe. There will be no option to hold on to the stock even if you believe it will go up in value soon.

Options have major pros and also major cons. You need to be aware of these before you step into the arena of options trading.

Put Options

On the other side of the options investment is the put option. Whereas call is the right to purchase, 'put' gives you the option to sell a certain security at a set price within a specific time frame. Investors usually purchase put options to protect the price of a stock in case it suddenly drops down, or even the market itself. With put options, you can sell the shares and your investment portfolio is protected from unexpected market swings. Put options are, therefore, a way to hedge your portfolio or lower its risk.

For example, you have invested in stock ABC for 100 shares, which you bought for $50 per share. As of May 31, the price per share has reached a market high $70. Of course, you'd want to maintain this position in your stock, and at the same time protect your gained profits in case the price of this stock goes down. To fit your requirements, you may purchase a put option with a three-month expiration and $70 per share strike price.

If ABC's stock price goes down drastically over the next couple of months, reaching a low per-share price of only $60, you will still be protected. By exercising your put option, you will still be able to sell the shares at $70 each even if stock ABC is now trading at a lower value. If you are feeling confident that ABC can still recover in the future, you can hold on to the stock and just resell the put option. The price of this put option will have gone up because of the diving stock ABC took.

On the other hand, if stock ABC's value kept climbing, just let the put option expire and you would still profit from the increased price of the shares. Even though you lost what you have invested in the put option, you still have the underlying stock with you. Therefore, you can view the put option as a kind of insurance policy for your investment, which may or may not use. Another thing to remember is that you can purchase put options even if you don't own the underlying stock, just like you would in a call option. You are not required to own the stock itself.

Risks Involved in Put Options

Just as with call options, put options carry the same risks. There is also a 100% loss potential when the underlying stock price goes up, and a huge gain when the price dives because you can resell the option for a higher price.

CHAPTER 5:

The Collar

The collar strategy is an extremely flexible way of trading that you can use for either short term or long-term positions. Mind you, when using it for long term positions, make sure you have substantial unrealized gains already present. This is because the collar imposes a maximum gain limit.

On the flip side, it also caps your downside loss, so this lends itself very well to short term speculative strategies. Mind you, when I say short term, I'm still talking about holding onto the position for at least a month to take advantage of the time decay. From a longer term investment perspective, if you have a position which has made you a lot of money but you're either unsure of how it's going to perform over the short term or are not sure if it will move much further over the long term, you can use the collar to squeeze out the last drops of income from the trade or let it take you out.

This strategy introduces an additional layer on complexity since it has three legs to it:

A long stock positions

A long protective or married put

A short-covered call

In essence, we're adding a long protective put to the covered call strategy. This helps cover the downside and adds to the advantages that a covered call has.

Execution

The first leg to establish is the long stock leg. Like with the covered call, this is an income generator and is entered with the thought of having it increase in value. The second leg to enter is the married put. A married put is a put that covers your downside. Think of it as a stop loss order. Your maximum loss is capped to this level.

The put is bought at an out of the money price (that is below current market levels) at a price that is equal to your maximum risk limit for that position. So, if you think you want to risk a move of just 5 points, then the put is purchased at that price.

Lastly, you need to write an out of the money call just like with the covered call. This call is covered by your long stock position. Make sure you execute your position in this exact order so that you minimize your risk. Let's work through the scenarios on this trade.

If your stock decreases in value, the put below it caps your maximum loss. Once the stock goes below the put's strike price, thereby moving it into the money, that leg is going to be in a profit no matter how low the stock's price goes. If you wish to exit, you sell your stock and you can sell your put which would have increased in value.

Alternatively, if the stock increases in value but doesn't hit your call's strike price before expiry, you earn the premium and the capital gain but are out the amount you paid to buy the put. If the stock does hit the call's strike price, this is your maximum gain possible on the stock leg and you'll have to sell your stock at the call's strike price.

In this case you again earn the capital gains on the long stock leg and the premium on the covered call leg but are out the premium you paid for buying the put. In addition to this, there are alternative scenarios you can encounter.

Let's say the stock declines in value but you're not sure that this is a long-term thing. You feel it's a temporary blip and it'll soon turn upwards. So, what do you do? Should you exit all three positions? Well, this is where the decision to adjust your trade comes into play. You can either reestablish the collar at different prices, which is change the strike prices of the call and the put, or you can exit altogether.

Technical and fundamental analysis should play a part in your decision. For now, just keep in mind that the collar is a wonderfully flexible strategy and with adjustment you can make money even when the trade goes against you or if something unexpected happens.

Now, let's look at an example with real numbers to see how it all plays out.

Example

Sticking with GOOG, we see that the market price is still $1229. So as a first step, in case this is a speculative position, we establish the long stock leg. Next, we establish the long put or protective put. Which price should you choose? Remember, this is an option purchase, so you'll need to pay to enter the position.

The temptation will be to enter at as low a price as possible since you're going to lose this money no matter what happens (if it moves into the money or remains out of the money you lose the option premium no matter what). Resist the temptation to look at this in monetary terms.

Instead look at it in terms of risk involved. Your put's strike price will dictate your maximum position size. You need to decide what your necessary risk per trade amount is going to be. This can be a function of either a percentage of your overall capital or a fixed amount.

Once this is done, you divide this amount by the points between your put and the long stock entry point and this gives you your position size. Simple math really. Place your put at a level beyond the closest support which you think is going to hold. The idea is to not have this put move into the money, not minimize the cost you pay.

Remember that this trade is only going to last a little beyond a month so don't go searching for the stronger support out there. Simply pick the most appropriate one given the current balance in the market. For example, if it's in a range, simply pick a level which is beyond the lower range boundary.

Let's say you decide to enter GOOG at the current market price and that an appropriate put level is 1200. Looking at GOOG's option chain, we see that the October 25th, 1200 put is selling for $25.20. So, this amount is going to go out of pocket, in addition to whatever you paid for the long stock.

Now, we search for an appropriate level to write our call. It is yielding the same price as before and that is $16. We will receive this amount no matter what.

Hence, our cost of entry equals:

Cost of entry = cost of long stock price + cost of put premium - premium received from short call = 1229+25.2-16 = 1238.20 per share

You'll notice how the cost on entry actually increases with this method as opposed to a straight long stock purchase. Well, this is the price you pay for the additional protection. If you were to merely protect your downside via a put, your breakeven price would increase by the value of the put premium. In this case, that works out to $25.20.

So, the covered call reduces your breakeven price quite significantly while maintaining your downside as intended. All in all, you pay a few dollars more for this privilege which is a good deal overall. Now that we know our cost of entry, what is our maximum loss?

Maximum loss = Long stock entry - Put strike price - premium from call + put premium paid = 1229-1200-16+25.2 = $38.20 per share.

If you placed a stop loss order at the put's strike price wouldn't that cover your downside for a lesser amount? Yes, but remember that the put insulates you from the possibility of the market price jumping your stop loss level thanks to a lack of liquidity or excess volatility. So, there is a price to pay for this protection. Let's see how your maximum gain is affected.

Maximum gain = Call strike price - Long stock entry price - put entry premium + call writing premium = 1270-1229-25.2+16 = $31.80 per share

In these calculations, the premiums you pay and receive for the options skew the numbers quite a lot. In reality, a lot of options strategies do not take the premiums paid into account when figuring out the maximum gain and risk because this is a cash expense. However, I'm illustrating these here just to show you how it affects the numbers.

So, it looks like you're risking a larger amount than what you stand to gain when you take the premiums into account. Two things about this: this is just an example and I've assumed certain price levels, so this is not fully reflective of the strategy. Second, this highlights the importance of picking a good put and call strike price level since the premiums do skew the numbers quite a lot.

This is why it's extremely important for you to brush up on your technical analysis skills prior to trading collars. You can get away with imperfect knowledge when it comes to the covered call since that has a large long stock leg which makes you all the money. However, over here your holding time is shorter, and your transaction costs are higher.

Hence, get to know the stock you're trading deeply and simulate collars on it before going live. The collar should really be the cornerstone of your options trading strategy so make sure you master this before moving onto the other strategies in this book. In terms of progression, I would say do not move ahead until you're making steady money with collars.

On the plus side, once you've established the collar, it needs no maintenance and pretty much takes care of itself. This doesn't mean you switch off from the market completely. I'd suggest checking in at least once a day, which is the minimum required for passive trading strategies.

The collar as you can see is a long-biased strategy. Is it possible to have a bearish collar? Well, yes, it is actually. Now that you've grasped the basics of the execution required as well as the math that underlies the strategy, let's look at what to do in case you wish to adjust the trade.

Adjustments

So, you've entered a collar and promptly the price dives below your entry and brings your put into the money. What now? You were envisioning holding onto the position for at least a month but here you are, less than a day in the trade, and you're already facing the prospect of hitting your maximum loss.

The first thing to do is to evaluate whether your technical assumptions are still valid. If your technical analysis was spot on, usually there will be some fundamental event you have overlooked. Is your stock dependent on the bond market, unbeknownst to you? Check your assumptions once again and see if your entry logic still holds water. If it doesn't, eat the loss and move on. Chalk it up to the cost of tuition of learning how to trade.

By the way, expect to do this sort of thing quite a lot when you're starting out. Trading is not an easy endeavor, and this is why you should make as many of your mistakes in simulation, while demoing your strategies, instead of jumping into a live account and sabotaging yourself.

Assuming your initial conclusions are still valid, perhaps this is a temporary downswing in an effort to shakeout the weaker long traders. In such cases, you can seek to reestablish your collar. First, sell your put position and determine what will be a more appropriate level to reenter. When you sell your put, you'll make money on that leg since it would have moved into the money.

CHAPTER 6:

Vertical Spread

When it comes to spread trading, there are two categories all types of trades fit into. These are vertical spreads and horizontal spreads. The names sound fancy but understanding how they work really isn't anywhere near as complicated.

Having said that, these types of trades do crank the complexity level up a bit. If the collar took things up a notch from covered calls then spread trades do the same with the collar. As beneficial as collars and covered calls are there is one major disadvantage that those strategies pose to the trader.

They require a long stock purchase. In the case of a covered call this is an investment while in the case of a collar it can be speculative or an investment. Whatever the designation there's no escaping the fact that long stock investment requires a lot of money. What if you wish to emulate Thales' example and get in on low capital values?

This is what the spread strategies address. Options give us the flexibility to play around with the way price moves and as you'll see, spread trades encompass taking advantage of a wide variety of market behavior.

Bull Call Spreads

The first type of vertical spread we'll be looking at is the bull call spread. This is a bullish trading strategy and works best in the middle portions of trending markets. I'll address why this is so. For now, keep in mind that while this is a bullish strategy it works best when bullishness is beginning to slow down, and you observe the ranges getting larger.

You can utilize this in the earlier, more forceful, part of trends but this isn't the most efficient use of it. In those portions, you're better off simply buying a call and letting its premium rise. The covered call works well in those environments too.

Either way, the bull call spread has two legs to it. You will be buying one call and selling another. Thus, the long call leg of the trade covers the short call. Let's take a look at the legs in more details

Trade Legs
The first leg you should establish is the long call leg. This needs to be an at the money or sightly out of the money call that you're sure will move into the money soon. The objective is to use this leg to make the majority of the profit in this trade. In essence, you're substituting the long stock position from the previous two strategies with a long call position.

Establishing a long stock position meant that you needed to protect it somehow which is why we had to incorporate a third leg in the case of the collar. With the covered call, given the investment nature of the trade, downside protection is moot since you'll be holding onto it for the long term anyway and the objective is to hold onto your investment no matter how much it dips (assuming the dip isn't catastrophic.)

The second leg of the bull call spread is the short call. This is written out of the money at a point where you think price will advance to, even if it does so sluggishly. Much like with every other strategy we've looked at, you want both of these options to expire at least 30 days or more from the trade date. This helps you capture and avoid the risk of time decay.

Like the collar, the bull call spread can be adjusted, and its greatest power lies in a good adjustment. This allows you to remain in the market at low cost. Adjustments depend on what the market scenario looks like. You should deploy this in times when bullishness is starting to be challenged by bearishness and thus, you will enter with the knowledge that the trend is still strong but there are some headwinds ahead.

You should place your short call at a level beyond the most relevant resistance ahead. Once price breaches this level, you should move it a few points higher to where the next resistance level could potentially be and so on. Alternatively, if you feel that the counter trend presence is becoming far too much, you could let the market take you out of the position and close your long and cover your short position.

Bull Put Spread

The bull put spread strategy seeks to take advantage of the exact same set of market conditions that the bull call spread seeks. So, what is the difference between the two? Aside from the obvious fact that one strategy uses calls and the other uses puts, there are many subtleties that you ought to be aware of.

The strategies do not contradict one another, in case you're wondering. Think of it as having two choices to pursue depending on what market conditions look like. If you're wondering how to determine the conditions which are ideal for each strategy, then the first step is to take a look at the bull put spread and understand how it works.

Trade Legs
Like the bull call, the bull put is a two-legged trade. The first leg involves establishing a long-put position which is out of the money and is below a strong support level. This long put is what caps your downside risk in case things go wrong. In addition to this, the long put also covers the next leg.

This is a short put which is written near or at the money. This leg is the primary profit driving instrument for the trade. I'd like to point out here that the structure and positioning of the puts is very different from that of the calls. With the bull call spread, you were capping your maximum gain on the trade by writing an OTM call.

Here's you're not capping any gains and are in fact capping your loss via a trade leg. In the bull call spread, your maximum loss was automatically capped as a part of the trade structure. You could argue that this is what is happening here as well but it's pretty clear that the way in which the strategies do this is very different.

The next major point of difference is in the results trade entry gives you. The bull call is net debit trade, but the bull put is a net credit trade. Net debit trades have you realize your maximum loss upon trade entry. Net credit trades realize your maximum gain upon entry. This means, you earn your maximum profit on entry and if all goes well, your options will maintain themselves.

Like the bull call spread, you can adjust the trade depending on market conditions. Given that your upside is not capped, adjustments will need to be made primarily if the market turns downwards and if you see your puts move into the money. In this case, you will need to readjust the spread lower and exit your primary position. Thus, the adjustment scenarios in the bull put strategy aren't as varied as they are in the others we've seen so far.

If the trade works in your favor, you can establish a higher spread using the same principles you used to establish the initial one.

Bear Call Spread

If you can use call spreads to take advantage of bullish conditions, you can use them to take advantage of bearish ones as well. In case you're wondering, it is possible to do this with puts as well and much like what we saw with the bullish spreads, you have a choice of using either call or put spreads to do this. For now, let's take a look at bear call spreads.

The bear call spread has two legs to it, much like the bull spreads do. As the name suggests you'll be setting up calls as part of this strategy. Let's take a deeper look at the two legs now.

Trade Legs

The first leg you want to establish is a long call position. The long call is placed at a level that is beyond a resistance zone and is the leg that limits your risk. The call itself is placed out of the money. The further away the call is, the greater your risk in the trade is.

The second leg to establish is the primary profit driving leg of this trade. This is a short call you will write as close to the money as possible. The exact placement of this level is a tricky thing since you don't want it to move into the money. If it does, you'll have to wind up both legs of the trade and take your maximum loss amount.

Bear call spreads are net credit trades which means you'll capture your entire gain upon trade entry. As such, like other options trading strategies we've seen thus far, you don't need to do anything special to maintain the trade. You can adjust it as well but given that this is a net credit trade, there isn't much you can do in terms of adjustment beyond working out another spread level in case the original trade doesn't work out.

Bear Put Spread

The bear put spread is the bearish cousin of the bull call spread in that it is a net debit trade that seeks to capture more of the upside in a bearish movement. By now, hopefully you've got a hang of how vertical spread trades are setup so let's quickly run through how this trade works.

Like the other three it has two legs to it: A long put and a short put. The long put is established at the money or as near to the money as possible and is the primary profit driver in this trade. The short put is written out of the money, a few levels below and functions as a profit target of sorts. The aim with this trade, like with the bull call spread is to capture as much of the market movement as possible. Hence, adjustments play an important role here. Once the market moves close to your short call, you can adjust your target downwards and move your long call leg up.

The timeline for this trade is the same as that of the others. You're looking at establishing options that are at least 30 days or so away from the trade entry date in order to avoid or capture as much of the time decay as possible. Using our TSLA example with a market price of $478.15, let's assume that we write the TSLA 450 option expiring a month from now.

This will net us $23.90 in premiums. We can go long on the 475 put which will cost us $36.05. Thus, the net debit on the trade and our maximum loss is $12.15. Our maximum gain is limited to the strike price of the OTM put and this is $25.

CHAPTER 7:

Horizontal Spread

Here are some horizontal spreads that traders should know about.

Calendar Call Spread Strategy

The spreads we've seen thus far have been what are called vertical spreads. This implies how they show up on the option chain, where strike prices are listed on top of one another. By shorting one and buying another, you're earning the difference in the prices of the two and hence the term' spread'.

Vertical spreads require you to trade options within the same expiration month but horizontal spreads, which is what the calendar spread is, involves buying and selling options form different expiration months. The call calendar spread is a bullish strategy that can be used to great effect as we'll see.

Execution

The calendar call spread consists of two legs:

A current month or short-term short call

A near month or longer-term long call

The idea is that while the stock takes its time to make it to the longer (time frame) call's strike price, you might as well collect the premium on the short call in the meantime. The instrument for profit is the longer call which captures the upward movement in the stock.

The longer-term call can be from the near month or something from the longer cycle. The choice is yours. The only consideration here is the liquidity since you don't want to be trading in an instrument which has a huge spread thanks to low demand or trading volume. As long as the liquidity is fine and spreads are low or manageable, you should be fine.

As your first step to implementing the trade, you will purchase an at or in the money call in anticipation of the move upwards. The short call is at a level you think the price is not going to reach within that time frame. The idea is to earn the premium from the short call and the capital gain from the long call. If this trade works out, it is as close to a win-win as you can get in the markets. Let's see how the math works with AMZN.

Let's say our long call is from the near month. The price we'll pay for the 1830 call, which is the one nearest to market price and in the money is $63.65. For our short call, let's say there a medium level resistance at 1840, which AMZN is going to have to work to get past and is unlikely to do this by the end of the month.

The premium we earn on this call is $36.30.

The cost of entry = Cost of long call - premium earned from short call = 63.65-36.3 = $27.35 per share.

Maximum loss = cost of entry

There are many scenarios for calculating the maximum gain as you can imagine since this depends on whether the short-term call ever moves into the money. Whatever the scenario, you will have to subtract your cost of entry from the final gain.

Horizontal spreads are thus different from vertical spreads thanks to their open-ended nature. It will take some getting used to, but with time, you'll find that they tend to be far more rewarding if you can get your analysis correct.

Put Calendar Spread

The horizontal put spread is similar in premise to the call calendar spread except it seeks to take advantage of a bearish market. The structure of the trade is also similar to call. It's just that you'll be buying puts instead of calls. There are two legs that are a part of the trade.

The short put leg is placed at a strike price that is beyond a support level that is medium in strength. It will have an expiry date that is beyond 30 days out but less than the expiry date of the second, long put leg. The long put will have the same strike price as the short put.

The idea is to capture the benefits of the short-term neutral behavior and the long-term bearishness. The shorter term, short put provides a premium and the long term put provides capital gains in the form of increases in intrinsic value as prices dive. This is also a net debit trade.

Much like the call calendar spread, the put spread can be adjusted as well depending on the type of market behavior observed. The most common adjustment methods involve converting it into a vertical spread to take advantage of price behavior.

This concludes our look at horizontal spread trades. As you can see, they're not very complex in nature and are far easier to maintain and understand than vertical spread trades. Spread trades are a step up from collars and like the collar, they offer decent and steady rewards when executed correctly.

CHAPTER 8:

Strangles and Straddles

D oing this requires some attention on your part. You are going to have to think ahead in order to implement this strategy and profit from it. Remember that you can use a straddle or strangle any time that you think the stock is going to make a major shift one way or the other. An example of a non-earning season situation, where this could be a useful strategy, would be a new product announcement. Think Apple. If Apple is having one of their big presentations, if the new phone that comes out disappoints the analysts, share prices are probably going to drop by a large amount. On the other hand, if it ends up surprising viewers with a lot of new features that make it the must-have phone again, this will send Apple stock soaring.

The problem here is you really don't know which way it's going to go. There are going to be leaks and rumors but basing your trading decisions on that is probably not a good approach, often, the rumors are wrong. A strangle or straddle allows you to avoid that kind of situation and make money either way.

Other situations that could make this useful include changes in management or any political interaction. We mentioned the government recently made a privacy settlement with Facebook. If you knew when the settlement was going to occur but wasn't sure what it was going to be, using a strangle or straddle might be a good way to earn money from the large price moves that were sure to follow.

The same events that might warrant buying a long call such as a GDP number or jobs report, for options on index funds, are also appropriate for strangles and straddles.

Implied Volatility Strategy

Implied volatility is very important when a big event like an earnings report is coming. This gives you a way to make profits. In fact, we are going to call this the implied volatility strategy.

Let's review how this would work. Remember, implied volatility is a projection of what the volatility of the stock is going to be in the near future. When there is an earnings call, the volatility is going to be extreme on the day after the call. Therefore, you are going to see the implied volatility growing as earnings day approaches.

At the time I am writing this, it is 24 hours before Facebook's earnings call. The implied volatility is 74%, which is very high. In contrast, for Apple, which is more than a week away from its next earnings call, the implied volatility is only 34%. This is for a $207.50 strike put, with a share price of $207.9.

The strategy is to profit from the implied volatility. You want to enter your position one to two weeks before the earnings call or big announcement. As implied volatility increases, this is going to swamp out time decay and cause a big rise in the option price.

Using that Apple put option, if we assumed that there were only 4 days to expiration, but the implied volatility had risen to about where Facebook is and there were no other changes (so we will leave the share price where it was), the price of the put option would increase by about $330.

So, if nothing else, you could profit from the change of implied volatility. It will probably go highest the day before the earnings call.

This is going to be magnified if you trade a strangle or straddle. Prior to the earnings call, both the put and the call option are going to increase a great deal in value because of implied volatility. So, you could sell the strangle the day before the earnings call and book some profits then. Since a strangle or straddle can earn big profits if there is a large move in the share price, you won't find any problems locating a buyer.

Estimating Price from Implied Volatility

If you know the implied volatility, you can make an estimate of the price range of the stock. This can be done using a simple formula.

(Stock price x implied volatility)/SQRT (days in a year)

If you don't want to do the calculation, if we take the square root of 365, it is about 19.1. For example, we use Facebook with a share price of $202.50 and an implied volatility of 76%.

Facebook	
Stock Price	$202.50
Implied Vol.	0.76
Days in a year	19.1049732
Expected Change	$8.06
Upper Range	$210.56
Lower Range	$194.44

The implied volatility gives us an idea of what traders are thinking, in regard to the upcoming earnings call, but of course, we can never be sure what is really going to happen until it does. But this gives us upper and lower bounds. Using the information that we have available, we can guess that Facebook might rise to $210.56 a share after the earnings call, or it might drop to $194.44 per share after the earnings call. You can use these boundaries to set up your strategy. However, remember that if there is a big surprise, it can go well past these boundary points in one direction or the other.

What is a Long Straddle?

To set up a straddle, you buy a put option and a call option simultaneously (buy = take a long position). The maximum loss that you can incur is the sum of the cost to buy the call option plus the sum of the cost to buy the put option. This loss is incurred when you enter the trade.

With a straddle, you buy a call option and a put option together. And they would be with the same strike price. By necessity, this means that one option is going to be in the money and one option is going to be out of the money. When approaching an earnings call, the prices can be kind of steep, because you want to price them close to the current share price. That way, it gives us some room to profit either way the stock price moves.

A maximum loss is only incurred if you hold the position to expiration. You can always choose to sell it early, if it looks like it's not going to work out and take a loss that is less than the maximum.

There is a total premium paid for entering into the position. This is the amount of cash paid for buying the call added to the money paid for buying the put. This is called the total premium. There are two breakeven points:

To the upside, the breakeven point is the strike price + total premium paid.

On the downside, the breakeven point is the strike price − total premium paid.

It the price of the stock moves up past the breakeven point, the put is worthless. However, the call option would earn substantial profits. On the other hand, if the stock price moved down past the lower price point, that would be the breakeven, the call option would be worthless and the put option would earn substantial profits.

For example, suppose that we buy a $207.5 straddle on Apple 7 days to expiration with an implied volatility of 35%, and the underlying price is $207. The total cost to enter the position is $8.03 ($803 total). At 1 day to expiration, the share price breaks up to $220 a share after the earnings call. The put expires worthless, but the call jumps to $12.50. The net profit is then $12.50 - $8.03 = $4.47, or $447 in total per contract.

If instead, the share price had dropped to $190, the call expires worthless, and the put jumps to $17.50 per share. The net profit, in this case, is then $17.50 - $8.03 = $9.47 per share or a total of $947.

This isn't to say that the straddle would be more profitable for a stock decrease, it is not. The profit will be the same no matter which way the share price moves, in our examples, we used two different sized moves. The point is to illustrate that no matter which direction the stock moves, you can profit.

If the stock is at the money at expiration, we could still recoup some of the investment and sell the straddle for a loss. In this case, the call and the put would both be priced at $152. We'd still be at a loss, but we could recoup $304 by selling both at $152.

Short Straddle

If you sell a straddle, then you are taking the opposite position, which means you would be betting that the share price stays inside the range and hope that the stock didn't make a big move to the upside or the downside. To sell a straddle you'd have to either be able to do a covered call and protected put or be a level 4 trader who could sell naked options.

Long Strangle

A strangle is similar to a straddle, but in this case, the strike prices are different. In this case, you will buy a just barely out of the money call option, while simultaneously buying a slightly out of the money put option. The two options will have the same expiration date. The breakeven points for a strangle are going to be calculated in a similar way as the breakeven prices for a straddle, but you are going to use the individual strike prices for the call and put because they are different. So, you calculate the total premium paid, which is the total amount paid for the call option plus the premium paid for the put option. Then the breakeven points are given by the following formulas:

To the upside, the breakeven point is the strike price of the call + total premium paid.

On the downside, the breakeven point is the strike price of the put – total premium paid.

In a similar fashion as compared to a long straddle, the maximum loss is going to occur when the share price ends up in between the two strike prices. Therefore, you might want to choose strike prices that are relatively close, in order to minimize the range over which the loss can occur. Of course, there is a tradeoff here because the closer in range the strike prices are, the more expensive it is going to be in order to enter the position. But, it's going to increase your probability of profit because if the strike prices are tight about the current share price, there is a higher probability that the share prices are going to exceed the call strike + premium paid, or decrease below the put strike price less the price paid to enter the contract (the premium).

CHAPTER 9:

Greeks

When you begin options trading, you are going to encounter some mysterious parameters called "the Greeks." These are five pieces of data that accompany every option, and they are denoted with Greek letters. The designations used are a result of the mathematical formulas that go into options pricing, but don't let that put you off. In reality, the Greeks are pretty straightforward, and you don't have to follow all of the Greeks in your analysis of what options to trade. Many options traders don't pay much attention to the Greeks, but as a more informed options investor, you are going to want to, at least, be aware of them and check their values.

Greeks Change in Real-Time

The first thing to know about the Greeks before we get started looking at them in detail is that they change in real-time. So, if someone tells you that delta is 0.5 or 0.62, it doesn't mean these are going to be the values that you see by the time you look at the option. As the stock trades all day long, and the value of the share price changes, the values of the Greeks are going to change as well. The magnitude of those changes may or may not be small, depending on what is going on with the markets. This is just something to keep in mind and to be aware of as we discuss each of the Greeks.

As we go about discussing the Greeks, I am going to be listing them in the order of importance as I see it. Not all options traders will agree, so you can take my listings with a bit of a grain of salt. But nonetheless, this will help you to understand what they are, their meaning, and how important they are to your trading.

Delta

The first Greek that we are going to encounter is named for the Greek letter delta. This parameter tells you how the price of an option is going to change with respect to a change in the share price of the underlying stock. It is listed as a decimal number that ranges from 0.0 – 1.0.

The dividing line for delta is 0.50, which is the value delta would have for an option that was exactly at the money. So, what does this mean? It means that if the price, for instance, goes up by an increment of $1.00, you are looking at a call option that is $0.50 more. So, if the share price of Disney happened to be $132, and you possess a call option having the exact price, if the share price went up to $132.50, the price of the call option would go up by $0.25. On the other hand, if the share price had risen to $133, the value of the call option would have risen by $0.50.

While traders like to focus on gains, this cut both ways. So, if the stock dropped from $132 a share to $131 a share, your option would drop in value by $0.50.

Remember that options prices are quoted on a per-share basis, but they are for 100 shares of stock. That means that a 50-cent drop is quite significant. If you're looking at an option that is priced at $100, a 50 cent drop in share price could translate into a drop in the price of the option of $25. And of course, if it rose by $0.50, you'd make $25 on the option.

Put options have a negative delta. This reflects the fact that the correlation between the put's value and the fluctuation in the share's price is in the opposite manner. That is, if the price of the stock goes up, the put option loses value. If it's another way around; that is, the stock loses its favorable spot in the market, the put options become lucrative when traded. But the meaning is the same.

So, when you are looking at an at the money put option, you are going to see a delta of -0.50. If the price of the stock rises by $1, you will lose fifty cents per share on the option. In contrast, if the stock dropped by $1 in value, you would gain fifty cents.

If an option is deemed to be "in the money," it creates a favorable condition, with the delta having a value of 0.50+. We can say that the delta responds well to the money conditions. Remember that delta's value goes up the more the option reaches the in the money condition. If Disney is trading at $130.50, we find that a $129 call option has a delta of 0.7149. A $122 call has a delta of 0.9449.

Theta

The second Greek that you want to keep an eye on is theta. This is a measure of time decay for the option. Theta is always negative. This reflects the fact that as time goes on, the value of the option that is tied up in time value declines. The time value of an option always declines; the question is only by what amount. You can look up theta to determine the amount. As stocks are traded throughout the day, the value of theta is going to change. However, the way that you are going to feel theta is when the days pass. So, at each market open on a new trading day, options will lose extrinsic value. The amount of value that they lose will be equal to the value of theta.

If you look up an option that is priced at $1 (per share), and you see theta is -0.11, at market open, the value of the option will drop to $0.89. In real terms, if you had bought the option for $100, it would drop in value to $89.

That illustrates how theta works. It's going to make its impact felt at the market open. Options do not lose time value during the day; it's the number of days to expiration that is important. The fewer the number of days left to expiration, the less time value the option has. As it loses value each day, we say that the option is experiencing time decay. All options go through time decay, no matter what. Since it's the number of trading days left to expiration that determines this, it only applies as the market opens.

However, time decay is not the only thing impacting options pricing. Suppose that delta for some call option that was $1 at the previous market close is 0.65, and theta is -0.11. If the share price were to rise a dollar at market open, that means delta and theta would add up to determine the new options price. So, it would go up 65 cents from delta but drops 11 cents from theta. So, you would have a net increase of 54 cents, and the option would now be priced at $1.54.

This exercise illustrates the fact that in order to estimate the future price of an option, you need to know everything that's going on. Even if there was no increase in share price at the market open, you might ignore the 11-cent drop. That's because it is going to be the only drop due to theta throughout the coming trading day, and a lot can happen throughout the day. A small move in stock price can easily make up for the drop in price due to time decay, and by the middle of the day, you might not even notice that you had lost that $11 off the value of the option.

However, you definitely need to account for that loss, so theta is not something to ignore. If the option is out of the money, it's going to be harder to make up for the value lost in the option due to time decay.

Vega

The third most important Greek (in my opinion) is vega. This Greek parameter tells you how sensitive the option is to changes in implied volatility. Precisely, the value of vega estimates how the price of the option is going to change in response to a 1% change in the implied volatility of the underlying stock. Under normal conditions, vega may not be that important. While you can look up the volatility for a given stock by looking at its beta parameter (note that beta is for the stock itself, not for options), that gives you the long-term volatility of the stock. Over short time periods, under most conditions, the volatility is not going to change all that much.

Before the earnings call, nobody knows for certain which way the shares are going to move. People will be engaging in a lot of speculation, but that speculation could be wrong. Furthermore, even if there is an earnings report that is good or bad, nobody can be quite sure how the market is going to react. Sometimes, the market won't react at all. But that doesn't matter prior to the earnings call because it's the implied volatility that we are concerned about when it comes to options.

As such, in the two weeks prior to an earnings call, you will see options prices spike from increases in implied volatility, and this phenomenon will reach a maximum right before the earnings call. You can profit from this by purchasing options a week or two prior to the calls and selling them when prices have risen enough to make the levels of profits that you are looking for.

So implied volatility is one thing to keep in mind when trading options. It is not always going to be significant, but there are times, like in earnings calls, when you are going to want to pay more attention to it and possibly utilize it in your trading strategy.

Rho

Next, we come to rho, which is a Greek parameter related to the risk-free interest rate. As we touched on in the first part, the risk-free interest rate is usually taken to be the interest rate on a 10-year U.S. Treasury bill. What is important for options is not the interest rate itself but how it is changing. Rising interest rates can make options less attractive because capital tends to leave the stock market and go into bonds when interest rates are rising by large amounts. In today's environment, and, in fact, over the past 20 years, this hasn't been too much of a concern. Interest rates have been at record low levels over the past decade, as government officials have been trying to use low-interest rates to prop up the economy. Whether that actually works or not is not our concern here, but the fact of the matter is they have only tentatively raised interest rates at times that they have considered doing so, which means that the impact on the stock market has been minimal.

Gamma

The final Greek is called gamma. Simply put, or maybe not simply put if you are not mathematically minded, gamma is the rate of change of delta. Technically, it's the second derivative. It tells you how rapidly delta is going to change with changes in stock prices. While hardcore options traders are going to be paying attention to this, most options traders don't need to keep a close eye on gamma. Beginning options traders are probably only going to be looking at delta and theta, and my experience is that delta provides the real information that you need when it comes to the sensitivity of the option to changing stock prices. Rather than following gamma, you are better off keeping tabs on the delta in real-time. The odds are that delta is not going to change much unless there is a very large change in stock prices.

CHAPTER 10:

Technical Analysis

Characteristics of Technical Analysis

This analysis makes use of models and trading rules using different price and volume changes. These include the volume, price, and other different market info.

Technical analysis is applied among financial professionals and traders and is used by many option traders.

The Principles of Technical analysis

Many traders on the market use the price to come up with information that affects the decision you make ultimately. The analysis looks at the trading pattern and what information it offers you rather than looking at drivers such as news events, economic and fundamental events. Price action usually tends to change every time because the investor leans towards a certain pattern, which in turn predicts trends and conditions.

Prices Determine Trends

Technical analysts know that the price in the market determines the trend of the market. The trend can be up, down, or move sideways.

History Usually Repeats Itself

Analysts believe that an investor repeats the behavior of the people that traded before them. The investor sentiment usually repeats itself. Due to the fact that the behavior repeats itself, traders know that using a price pattern can lead to predictions.

The investor uses the research to determine if the trend will continue or if the reversal will stop eventually and will anticipate a change when the charts show a lot of investor sentiment.

Combination with Other Analysis Methods

To make the most out of the technical analysis, you need to combine it with other charting methods on the market. You also need to use secondary data, such as sentiment analysis and indicators.

To achieve this, you need to go beyond pure technical analysis, and combine other market forecast methods in line with technical work. You can use technical analysis along with fundamental analysis to improve the performance of your portfolio.

You can also combine technical analysis with economics and quantitative analysis. For instance, you can use neural networks along with technical analysis to identify the relationships in the market. Other traders make use of technical analysis with astrology.

Other traders go for newspaper polls, sentiment indicators to come with deductions.

The Different Types of Charts Used in Technical Analysis

Candlestick Chart

This is a charting method that came from the Japanese. The method fills the interval between opening and closing prices to show a relationship. These candles use color coding to show the closing points. You will come across black, red, white, blue, or green candles to represent the closing point at any time.

Open-high-low-close Chart (OHLC)

These are also referred to as bar charts, and they give you a connection between the maximum and minimum prices in a trading period. They usually feature a tick on the left side to show the open price and one on the right to show the closing price.

Line Chart

This is a chart that maps the closing price values using a line segment.

Point and Figure Chart

This employs numerical filters that reference times without fully using the time to construct the chart.

Overlays

These are usually used on the main price charts and come in different ways:

• Resistance – refers to a price level that acts as the maximum level above the usual price

• Support – the opposite of resistance, and it shows as the lowest value of the price

• Trend line – this is a line that connects two troughs or peaks.

• Channel – refers to two trend lines that are parallel to each other

• Moving average – a kind of dynamic trendline that looks at the average price in the market

• Bollinger bands – these are charts that show the rate of volatility in a market.

• Pivot point – this refers to the average of the high, low, and closing price averages for a certain stock or currency.

Price-based Indicators

These analyze the price values of the market. These include:

• Advance decline line – this is an indicator of the market breadth

• Average directional index – shows the strength of a trend in the market

• Commodity channel index – helps you to identify cyclical trends in the market

• Relative strength index – this is a chart that shows you the strength of the price

• Moving average convergence (MACD) – this shows the point where two trend line converge or diverge.

- Stochastic oscillator – this shows the close position that has happened within the recent trading range

- Momentum – this is a chart that tells you how fast the price changes

Technical Analysis Secrets to Become the Best Trader

To make use of technical analysis the right way, you need to follow time-testing approaches that have made the technique a gold mine for many traders. Let us look at the various tips that will take you from novice to pro in just a few days:

Use More than One Indicator

Numbers make trading easy, but it also applies to the way you apply your techniques. For one, you need to know that just because one technical indicator is better than using one, applying a second indicator is better than using just one. The use of more than one indicator is one of the best ways to confirm a trend. It also increases the odds of being right.

As a trader, you will never be 100 percent right at all times, and you might even find that the odds are stashed against you when everything is plain to see. However, don't demand too much from your indicators such that you end up with analysis paralysis.

To achieve this, make use of indicators that complement each other rather than the ones that clash against each other.

Go for Multiple Time Frames

Using the same buy signal every day allows you to have confidence that the indicator is giving you all you need to know to trade. However, make sure you look for a way to use multiple timeframes to confirm a trend. When you have a doubt, it is wise that you increase the timeframe from an hour to a day or from a daily chart to a weekly chart.

Understand that No Indicator Measures Everything

You need to know that indicators are supposed to show how strong a trend is, they won't tell you much more. So, you need to understand and focus on what the indicator is supposed to communicate instead of working with assumptions.

Go with the Trend

If you notice that an option is trading upward, then go ahead and buy it. Conversely when the trend stops trending, then it is time to sell it. If you aren't sure of what is going on in the market at that time, then don't make a move.

However, waiting might make you lose profitable trades as opposed to trading. You also miss out on opportunities to create more capital.

Have the Right Skills

It really takes superior analytical capabilities and real skill to be successful at trading, just like any other endeavor. Many people think that it is hard to make money with options trading, but with the right approach, you can make extraordinary profits.

You need to learn and understand the various skills so that you know what the market seeks from you and how to achieve your goals.

Trade with a Purpose

Many traders go into options trading with the main aim of having a hobby. Well, this way you won't be able to make any money at all. What you need to do is to trade for the money – strive to make profits unlike those who try to make money as a hobby.

Always Opt for High value

Well, no one tells you to trade any security that comes your way – it is purely a matter of choice. Try and go for high-value options so that you can trade them the right way. Make use of fundamental analysis to choose the best options to trade in.

Be Disciplined

When using technical analysis, you might find yourself in situations that require you to make a decision fast. To achieve success, you need to have strict risk management protocols. Don't base on your track record to come up with choices; instead, make sure you follow what the analysis tells you.

Don't Overlook Your Trading Plan

The trading plan is in place to guide you when things go awry. Coming up with the plan is easy, but many people find it hard to implement the plan the right way. The trading plan has various components – the signals and the take-profit/stop-loss rules. Once you get into the market, you need to control yourself because you have already taken a leap. Remember you cannot control the indicators once they start running – all you can do is to prevent yourself from messing up everything.

Come up with the trading rules when you are unemotional to try and mitigate the effects of making bad decisions.

Accept Losses

Many people trade with one thing in mind – losses aren't part of their plan. This is a huge mistake because you need to understand that every trade has two sides to it – a loss and a profit. Remember that the biggest mistake that leads to losses isn't anything to do with bad indicators rather using them the wrong way. Always have a stop-loss order when you trade to prevent loss of money.

Have a Target When You Trade

So, what do you plan to achieve today? Remember, trading is a way to grow your capital as opposed to saving. Options trading is a business that has probable outcomes that you get to estimate. When you make a profit, make sure you take some money from the table and then put it in a safe place.

How to Apply Technical Analysis

Many traders have heard of technical analysis, but they don't know how to use it to make deductions and come up with decisions that impact their trades. Here are the different steps to make sure you have the right decision when you use technical analysis.

Identify a Trend

You need to identify an option and then see whether there is a trend or not. The trend might be driving the options up or down. The market is bullish if it is moving up and bearish when it is moving down. As a trader, you need to go along with the trend instead of fighting it. When you fight against the trend, you incur unnecessary losses that will make it hard to achieve the rewards that you seek.

You also need to have good ways to identify the trend; this is because the market has the capacity to move in a certain direction. It is not all about identifying the direction of the trend but also when the trend is moving out of the trend.

So, how can you identify a trend the right way? Here are some tools to use so as to get the right trend:

• Using triangles that map major swings

• The Bill Williams Fractals indicator helps you to identify the trend

• Use the moving average

• Trend lines give you an idea of the direction of the trend

Once you identify the trend, the next step is to try and mark the support and resistance levels

2. Support and Resistance Levels

You need to understand the support and resistance levels that are within the trend. Use the Fibonacci retracement tool to identify these spots on the trend.

3. Look for Patterns

Patterns need to show you what to expect in a certain market. You can use candlesticks to determine the chart pattern.

CHAPTER 11:

Probable Tips and Suggestions to Try to Succeed with Options Trading

Becoming an options trader who consistently enjoys success in his endeavors is not just something that you find yourself achieving overnight. You require to spice the process by bringing in new ideas and concepts that may seem probable. When these tips are incorporated in the right way you will surely find yourself up the ladder of success with a lot of ease. This article will equip you with some of these tips that you may use to your advantage.

One of the key tips is in ensuring that you focus on the prices of the options. You realize that options grow more and more worthless as time goes by simply because at the end of it all they will finally expire. This is a characteristic shared by all the options, no exception. The majority of the option traders make the mistake of laying so much emphasis on studying the market as well as the stock. They usually make their decisions on whether to buy or sell their options based on this. They often forget the prices of these options. You should always focus on buying low-priced options and sell the high-priced options. Being able to differentiate the low-priced options from the cheap options in the market is one of the steps towards success in options trading. A low-priced option usually provides a very high return. Failure to consider this factor of options prices may just make you end up accumulating losses. When the options are well thought of and analyzed properly, they can be very rewarding.

Another tip is to ensure that you have the necessary tools to stay in the market. Your risk management strategies should be well outlined. Your option trade can turn out to be the most successful if you manage your risks appropriately. However, the majority of the option traders usually focus on the amount of money they plan on getting and forget the loses they risk accumulating. You realize that most of the decisions that you make in option trading will be influenced by this factor. As for the case of the amount of capital that you would invest, you would only risk investing that amount that you would bear to lose in case things worked against you. Most of the option trading strategies, however, are quite risky. But you can try out various risk management strategies so as to minimize loses as much as possible. Enormous loses have the potential of affecting you for even a whole month or even make you exit the trade.

Creating a good game plan that is quite quantifiable is a major tip in ensuring success in options trading. Make sure that the goals outlined in the strategy are quite clear and realistic. They should not set the bar too high or rather appear in achievable in any way. With a clear strategy, you are able to focus on the latter. Your strategy should also be strict in a way that asses all the aspects of your options trading. Ensure that you also exercise the virtue of discipline to your course so as you reap success in an options trade. Your game plan should also be quite flexible to accommodate the changing market patterns.

It is quite advisable to trade with a well-known stock or rather one that you are quite familiar with. By this, you are able to even predict the price movements of stock. This is usually a very crucial exercise that can reap your maximum benefits. You also do not have to go through a lot of struggles on analyzing the stock as you are already familiar with them. However, there is a need to ensure that you consistently do a lot of market research on the same to keep up with the changing trends. For well-known stock, the majority of them enjoy huge volumes and have the tendency to remain in the market for longer periods.

The other tip is on the choice of an options trade broker. It is wise to ensure that they offer you with quite affordable or rather user-friendly commissions. High commissions will affect your profitability as well as your strategy. Nonetheless, do not go for the low fee brokers if they are not in a position to offer you reliable services like better trading opportunities as well as saving you time. Failure to which you may end up losing much of your dollars due to their inefficiency. For online brokers, ensure that they have convenient methods or platforms that can enable easy transfer of money. This decision on the choice of a broker is a decision worth spending a lot of time on. The success of your trade highly depends on the broker you chose.

It is quite possible to think that your psychology does not play a key role in the options trade. Many options traders overlook this and end up making decisions that ruin their trades completely. This is quite common especially when you make huge losses and become emotional. This is very normal and expected but you should learn that any decision you make while in this state of mind may completely work against you. It is therefore advisable to learn how to react to such losses. Moreover, try as much as possible to combat the fear of losing. This may refrain you from enjoying huge profits that you could have earned in case you entered the trade.

Ensure that you take advantage of market volatility. Many new traders have the tendency to overlook this critical factor. They do forget that it is not always that options will reflect the move that a particular stock will take. It is advisable to understand how market volatility affects the implied price of the option. In the case where there are susceptible high market volatility and consecutive huge moves. It is quite advisable to use the straddle strategy. This refers to the buying of the call and the put option at a particular strike price for a given period of time. It usually has the advantage of providing limited risks.

CHAPTER 12:

Possible Errors to Avoid That Can Be Committed in Option Trading

When trading options, it is possible to lose money that you have invested, and it is therefore important to be aware of errors that can be made when trading. They include lack of a strategy in exiting the market, trading in options that are not liquid among other mistakes that will be comprehensively talked about below.

Buying into the Option of the Out-Of-The-Money Call Options

In the options market, buying into the out-of-money options is one of the most difficult means of making money. Such call options are always inviting to new traders for in most cases they are always less expensive than other options. What most new traders do that make them lose money is enacting this strategy only, which does not give successful, consistent gains.

Lack of a Strategy in Trading

When a trader does not have a strategy in entering and exiting the market, there is a high possibility to make losses. Without a strategy, a trader will not know when to make a trade, and with what amount of money. A chance may, therefore, pass you when you've got no plan for your trading. Before buying or selling an option, make a clear cut and concise plan, to avoid making mistakes when trading, that would have otherwise been avoided.

Lack of a Strategy in Exiting the Market

Some traders lack an exit plan suitable for when they are making losses and conversely when they are making profits. An exit plan is to provide a solution when you want to close a trade. Without one, you will not know the appropriate time to close down a trade, which may leave you open to making huge losses in the market, when you don't close the trade early enough and reversed profits to losses when the markets reverse.

Not Putting into Consideration, the Expiry Date

Not have a prediction made on the time frame that a trade will go may prove to be loss-making. In trading options, making a prediction on how long trade of an option will take is a key aspect. Factors such as reports on earnings are crucial in determining the expiry date. Traders may fail to make decisions on the correct expiry dates that correlate with the factor events, that makes their strategy to be useless at this point.

Having so Much Leverage on the Trades Made

Traders who are mostly used to trading in the stocks market make the mistake of buying options with way too much money that is needed for options. Options are classified as derivatives and they do not, therefore, cost as much as the options. Large sums of leverage are therefore not needed in this category in the market, a mistake that many traders from the stock market are susceptible to doing. This opens up their trade to many losses, stemming from the unnecessarily high amount of leverage on the trades, such that when a trade does not go as intended, their whole strategy crumbles.

Trading with the Less Expensive Options

Cheap options in the market, which some traders may prefer, turn out to be no money-making options. The mistake in trading in the cheap options is that they have low premiums, whose strike price will always be way above the cost going in the market or as well below the market costs. To counter such a difference in the prices, the trader is therefore forced to create a more drastic strategy to salvage the options traded. It is not a wise decision to always buy cheap options.

Indecision on Early Options

The indecision that plagues some traders on the early options is always uncalled for. On an early option, some traders do not buy and sell the options in the right manner, according to the rights that they are accorded by the buyers. The indecision is always rooted in a panic on what to do with the options. They do not know at what appropriate time to close their losing trades and let the gaining ones remain open, without panicking over the possibility of the market reversing and them making losses thereafter.

Trading with the Wrong Size of a Trade

The portfolios that some traders have do not always go hand in hand with the size of the trades that they make. In one case scenario, they can be risking too much in trading risky options, whereby if they make losses, their portfolios cannot cover them. On the other hand, they can be making a trade that is way too risky, where they lose on trades that would've made gains, and the portfolios are well capable of covering that, the most common case under this mistake is the traders risking all of their portfolios. They do not think about the question of whether they could afford to risk the amount of money traded if the trades made losses.

Maximizing on a Losing Trade

Maintaining a losing trade for a long period of time is one of the mistakes that traders are highly susceptible to making. Riding on a losing trade that will just result in losses is of no good. When the indicator shows high levels of losses, traders do not exit the trade, with prospects that the trade will reverse. They do not distinguish between losing trades that do not reverse and the ones that can have the possibility of reversing from proper analysis.

Trading in Options That Are Not Liquid

This is a mistake that costs traders when they want to close a losing trade and at the same time much money than if the option would have been liquid. An illiquid option does not give the leeway to buy and sell options in a quick manner, therefore exiting the market when the trader's desires become difficult. Most of the traders who trade in options that are not liquid do not often check on the opening interest on the option. Most of the options that are illiquid will have less interest, thus less flexible that these with larger interests, usually the larger companies.

CHAPTER 13:

Simple Strategies to Use

Why use stock market strategies?

Here is a good question. Why is it worth using stock market strategies? You need to know that the financial instruments you are trading on, such as CFDs (contracts for difference), are already designed to be simplified and accessible for investment.

Even the platforms where you will find yourself performing from a practical point of view, your trading operations are very intuitive and can, therefore, be exploited both by industry experts who demand the possibility of trading professionally, via beginners who may never have put to this kind of tools but still want to create a monthly income by investing in the stock market.

One of the right reasons why it is worth learning the stock market strategies lies in the fact that we are sure that you too have always dreamed of finding a job that would not force you to move for long stretches, perhaps remaining stuck in traffic and city chaos, a job that does not oblige you to say yes to the boss on duty who may not even deserve to occupy that place, a job where you should not be forced to work overtime to be able to reach the end of the month charging you with stress and fatigue.

This is why we believe that trading with stock market strategies is the best possible alternative, not only offline but also online. Being independent in this promising world guarantees you the possibility to shake off the problems linked to the crisis to earn your freedom, even before the money, to become the master of your own life.

A thousand good reasons to trade with the right strategy

If you find yourself somehow, you have heard about the possibility of trading on the stock exchange, and maybe you know there is no way to do it online. If you want to take this path, we ask you not to feel intimidated or frightened by your possible future as a financial operator.

The stock exchange trading online has become a beginner or beginner's measure that it is. If, until today, you have only played lowly professions and do not have a higher degree, perhaps you think that you are not up to this kind of activity.

Perhaps you believe that the Stock Exchange and Markets, as well as the strategies to earn money, are beyond your means! Enough of this loser mentality.

The truth is that you are second to none, and you have the potential to be on a par with others and, why not, also to excel, especially in a world where meritocracy reigns like that of the stock market and financial markets on the internet.

Millions of people around the world have chosen the path of investment of their online capital, albeit very small. Now you can do it yourself by putting into practice the stock market strategies that we will propose to you during this guide.

Apply the right bag techniques

Do you think that all these people know every single nation and all the secrets of the financial markets to be able to earn a salary at the end of the month in this kind of activity?

This is not the case. Anyone who makes money from online trading does so from little to useful knowledge. It is, therefore, not a question of quantity; it is only a question of quality.

Few but good stock market strategies will allow you to become an established and successful trader who can afford to buy whatever he wants, in total independence, and without having to ask anyone for anything.

It is necessary to know as well as to apply the right bag technique. Learn it first through theory, then put it into practice in the field of trading, testing it continuously and optimizing it based on your trading methodology.

Do not miss the topics to come and immediately discover the best stock exchange strategies, the path that will lead you to become a real trader may be extended and tortuous, but in the end it will be worth it, and you will finally feel satisfied in an occupation free from conditioning and the harassment of the world of work as it has always known it.

If you start trading today, your old life will already be in the past, because you're about to be immersed in a virtuous circle of real opportunities to become an ace of stock trading. Cheers!

Difference Between Tactics and Stock Market Strategies

Modern stock exchange strategies have been devised to permanently change the old canons of traditional investment that made everything too slow and stiff, too challenging to apply, and this caused traders many problems and dissatisfactions, so much that many were eventually led to abandon this promising activity.

With the new strategies, the goal has been to make trading affordable and feasible for everyone, the doors are wide open, and anyone who wants it today can enter without suffering the typical problems of the past.

What it takes to make the most of the strategies that we propose to you in all respects is only basic knowledge of the subject of trading. Consequently, you are not called to know everything to start earning.

Therefore, trading does not mean having a degree in economics. After all, those who would be prepared today to face 5 years of studies to earn money, it is really too much time and too much sacrifice to put in place, so the techniques that you have to use to earn are simple but effective strategies that guarantee the success of the trades in most cases.

But because in stock trading, we talk about strategies and not tactics and because the former is much more successful and secure than the latter. The speech is very simple, and we want to clarify it with the following short definitions:

Investment Strategies

The strategy is the description of a long-term action plan used to set and subsequently coordinate all the actions that serve to achieve a particular, specific purpose. Strategies can be applied in all fields to reach the goal.

They, therefore, carry out the task of obtaining greater security by making a series of separate operations that help to reach an end goal. In the case of trading, we are talking about profit, which is undoubtedly the only primary aim that drives people to enter this business.

The simple tactic, on the other hand, is a course of action adopted according to the achievement of specific objectives, but in this case, we speak of small achievements in the short-term.

Adopting tactics would not be effective or satisfactory in the field of trading because it is not a structured plan, but simple plans to achieve small temporary objectives. In short, with a tactic you can also win a battle, but not war; winning a war requires a broader STRATEGY.

What all traders aim to achieve is a constant and lasting success over time that gives total security of a monthly income and specific collections on an annual basis. In stock exchange trading, it is possible to achieve all this by using strategies. Without strategies, you might perish as a trader very soon.

Applying stock exchange strategies requires attention and many precautions, especially at the beginning, when you are not much of an expert. In certain situations, when the markets become uncertain or careless, you do not know how to act, and you risk making mistakes.

At specific errors, however, the strategies cannot be remedied; in those cases, it will be the experience to act as a master and to suggest the right moves to make.

How much do you earn if you use the best strategy to invest?

With financial instruments available today, profit margins are simply impressive; operating in the right way, you can earn a lot of money even on a daily basis, but at that point, you have to take into account other factors such as the skill of the trader, the ability to avoid the losses, the amount of capital you have available, but also the small strokes of luck that from time to time can help to increase profits.

The amount of money that can be earned then also depends, above all, on the financial product you intend to use. There are not very marked differences but still tangible, depending on whether you prefer to trade forex, CFD, or investing in social trading.

Stock Market Strategies and Money Management

If you intend to trade on the stock exchange, there is no doubt that you will, sooner or later, have to come into contact with the rules of money management or all that concerns the management of money and your precious investment capital.

Money Management shows you the way to correct money management, so it is fundamental in trading, but its rules are also applied in other fields that are as varied as in the domestic or business economy. Ultimately, the rules it dictates are quite simple and due to pure and simple common sense, but in any case, it will be necessary to observe them religiously to avoid running into severe problems in your career as a trader.

The creators of the first money management techniques had a clear idea that it was necessary to produce a new awareness of the use of money in their investments, for the first time imposing the concept of diversification and differentiation of the investment portfolio to reduce the risks of trading and losses on investment capital drastically.

A strategic approach to stock exchange trading cannot, therefore, ignore the knowledge of the fundamental precepts of money management that require you to always establish the spending limit and the budget available at the beginning.

In the field of trading, this will mean establishing the risks that you are willing to run within certain limits that not even an "Indiana Jones" of trading could ever think of crossing; otherwise, it would face economic suicide at the speed of light! The principles of money management help you put both the risks and the potential profits on the scales to understand if a particular movement on the markets should be exploited or not; in other words, it helps you to know if the game is worth the candle.

If you learn to put the rules of money management into practice, your long-term success can be practically assured, but even the short and medium-term will be more probable and easily accessible. In short, all this talk turns to a need for investment efficiency.

The best traders are those who can minimize losses, which not even the guru of the economy could ever avoid and increase profits more and more.

The key to all this is precisely the fact that before learning to earn aspiring traders, the importance of learning to lose should be taught! Suffering losses and spilling money is a natural thing in trading, and you have to try to understand it and not give too much weight when a loss occurs.

The main rule of money management states that you should never, never, ever put at risk more than 5% of the total capital available in single trading operation.

Doing so would be stupid because it means that in case of loss, you should lose a lot of time trying to recover the negative position if you succeed. Furthermore, it is necessary to avoid losing more than 30% of the total capital available in a single trading day.

You simply have to recognize that when a bad day happens, you have to have the courage to turn off the computer or the device that you used to use to go for a nice walk and not run any further risk because it is clear that that day or you are not able to operate correctly or things in some way always row against you. It is the case to abandon the current session as soon as possible.

CHAPTER 14:

Tips for Options Traders

This is a much better and more successful strategy. Here are some helpful tips and advice that should guide you as you trade online in options.

1. The Price of Any Stock Can Move in 3 Basic Directions

These directions are up, down, and no movement at all. Depending on the kind of call that you have, you can leverage this movement to make a profit or at least avoid incurring losses.

Plenty of first-time traders and investors assume that prices of securities will go either up or down. However, this is a wrong school of thought because sometimes there is no movement at all in the price of stocks and shares. This is a very important fact in the world of options trading.

There are plenty of real-life, practical examples that show a particular stock or share which did not move significantly for quite a lengthy period. For instance, the KOL share traded within a $4 range for a total of 23 days. If you had invested money in either a call option or a put option through this stock, you would have lost money.

According to seasoned traders, chances of making a profit with a call or put option are hardly ever 50% but only 33%. This is likely due to the fact that stock price movements are random. You will eventually realize that 33% of the time, stocks rise; 33% of the time, they dip in price; and another 33% of the time, they stay the same. Time will more often be your worst enemy if you have a long put or call option.

A purchase of a call option is usually with the hope that prices will go up. In the event that prices do rise, then you will make a profit. At other times, the prices will remain the same or even fall. In such events, if you have an out-of-the-money call, the option will most likely expire, and you will lose your investment. In the event that the price remains stagnant and you have an in-the-money option, then you will at least recoup some of the money you invested.

There will be sometimes when frustrations will engulf you. This is when you just sit and watch prices start to skyrocket just a couple of weeks after the options you purchased had expired. This is often an indicator that your strategy was not on point and you did not give it sufficient time. Even seasoned traders sometimes buy call options that eventually expire in a given month and then the stocks prices rise sharply in the following month.

It is therefore advisable to purchase a longer-term call option rather than one that expires after a single month. Now, since stocks move in 3 general directions, it is assumed that close to 70% of options, traders with long call and put options suffer losses. On the other hand, this implies that 70% of option sellers make money. This is one of the main reasons why conservative options traders prefer to write or sell options.

2. Before Buying a Call or Put Option, Look at the Underlying Stock's Chart

Basically, you want to find out as much information as possible about the performance and worth of an underlying stock before investing in it.

You should, therefore, ensure that you take a serious look at the chart of the stock. This chart should indicate the performance of the stock in the last couple of days. The best is to look at a stock's performance in the last 30 and 90 days. You should also take a look at its last year's performance.

When you look at the charts, look at the movement of the shares and try and note any trends. Also, try and observe any general movement of the shares. Then answer a couple of questions. For instance, is the stock operating within a narrow range? Or is it bending upwards or downwards? Is this chart in tandem with your options trading strategy?

To identify the trend of a particular stock, try and draw a straight line along in the middle of the share prices. Then draw a line both above and below so as to indicate a channel of the general flow of the share.

Chart Readings and Buying Call Options

Let us assume that you wish to invest in a call option. Then you should ask yourself if the stock price is likely to rise and why. If you think that the stock will rise and trade at a higher level, then you may be mistaken, unless something drastic happens or new information becomes evident. New information can be a shareholders' meeting, impending earnings announcement, a new CEO, product launch, and so on.

If there is a chart showing the presence of support at lower prices and stock prices fall to that level, then it may be advisable to buy call options. The call option will be a great bet when prices are down because prices will very likely head back up. However, never allow greed to occupy your mind. When you see a profit, take and do not wait too long.

Chart Readings and Buying Put Options

Now, supposing the stock chart indicates a solid resistance at a higher price. If the stock is beginning to approach this higher level, then it is possible that the price might begin to move in that direction as well. So as the price moves, expect to gain small but significant profits. Avoid greed, so anytime the stock price falls, simply move in and make some money.

Chart Readings for Purchase of Call and Put Options

Now, if your chart readings indicate that the shares are within the lower levels of its range, then it is likely that daily changes in price will send it towards the middle of the range. If this is so, then you should move in and make a profit as soon as the price tends upwards. Even minor profits such as buying at $1 and selling at $1.15 mean a 15% profit margin.

3. Find Out the Breakeven Point Before Buying Your Options

Now, you need to identify a call option that you wish to invest in, especially after studying its performance on the market. Before buying, however, you should work out the breakeven point. In order to find this breakeven point, you will have to consider things such as the commissions charged and the bid spread.

It is very important that you are positive that the underlying stock of your options will move sufficiently so as to surpass the breakeven point and earn a tidy profit. You should, therefore, learn how to work out the breakeven point in options trade.

Calculating the Breakeven Point

As an options trader, you need to know how to calculate and find the breakeven point. In options trading, there are basically 2 break-even points. With short term options, you need to make use of the commission rates and bid spread to work out the breakeven point. This is if you intend to hold on to the options until their expiration date.

Now, if you are seeking short-term trade without holding on to the options, then find out the difference between asking price and bid price. This difference is also known as the spread.

4. If You Are Dealing with Call and Put Options, Embrace the Underlying Stock's Trend

As an investor and trader in options, you need to consider the trend of the underlying stock as your friend. This means that you should not fight it. Basically, if the stock price is headed upwards, you should find a strategy that is in tandem with this movement. If you oppose it, you are unlikely to win.

Similarly, if the stock is on a downward trend, then do not oppose this movement but try and find a strategy that will accommodate this trend. You need to understand, however, that this saying is intended to guide you but is not necessarily a rule. This means that you apply it even while you consider all other factors. For instance, the major news may have an immediate effect on the price trend of a stock or shares.

As a trader, you should learn to jump successfully on a trend and follow the crowds rather than go to extremes and oppose it. Most amateurs who see an upward trend often think the stock is about to level out. However, the reality is that the momentum is often considered a great thing by seasoned traders. Therefore, do not try and oppose the trend because you will surely lose. Instead, try and design a strategy that will accommodate the trend. In short, the trend is always your friend, do not resist, and momentum is truly great.

5. When Trading Options, Watch Out for Earnings Release Dates

Call and put options are generally expensive with the price increases significantly if there is an earnings release announcement looming. The reason is that the anticipation of very good or very bad earnings report will likely affect the stock price. When this is an underlying stock in an options trade, then you should adjust your trades appropriately.

Once an earnings release has been made, then options prices will fall significantly. You need to also watch out very carefully for this. The prices will first go up just before the earnings release and then fall shortly thereafter. It is also possible for call options prices to dip despite earnings announcements. This may happen if the earnings announced are not as impressive as expected.

As an example, stocks such as Google may rise insanely during the earnings announcement week only to dip significantly shortly thereafter. Consider Apple shares that were trading at $450 at the markets. Call options with Apple as the underlying stock were trading at $460. However, the market had targeted a price of $480 within 3 days, which did not happen. This cost investors' money. Such underlying assets are considered volatile due to the high increase in price, rapid drop shortly thereafter and related risk of losing money.

Additional Tips for Advanced Options Traders

One of the best pieces of advice for all advanced options traders specifically and all other traders, in general, is investing in education. Some of the most crucial trading techniques involve evaluating stocks, conducting fundamental analysis as well as performing technical analysis. You also need to be able to make decisions regarding the impending and future movement of security.

Options can be risky, and time is always against you. As such, you should be able to predict and foretell as accurately as possible the impending and future direction of an individual stock and the overall trend of the market.

Advanced Stock Options

Stock options are very similar to futures contracts. They also closely resemble ordinary stocks. However, they are all inherently different. As such, options can be viewed as contracts. Therefore, anytime a trader deals in options, they are dealing in a contract referencing an underlying security. This is basic information that all stock traders are aware of but is essential for refreshing the memory. Keep your eyes on technical analysis: Even before you begin any form of trading, you should refresh your memory on options trading. You also need to ensure that you have an appropriate strategy that will lead you to profitability. Technical analysis will point the direction that you'd expect your stocks or security to follow. It will help you come up with a strategy as well as the stock to pick.

113

CHAPTER 15:

Differences Among Forex, Stocks and Options

There is a wide range of trading options available today in the market. In fact, most of us get confused while choosing the one on which we should invest our capital. We will be talking about some of the major differences between forex, stocks, and options.

Forex and Options

Forex trading, often known as FX trading or Foreign Currency Exchange, is basically a market of finances where any person can easily trade the national currencies for making certain amounts of profits. Perhaps some people feel that the U.S. dollar will actually be stronger when compared to the British pound or euro. You can easily develop a strategy for affecting this form of trade and if your research turns out to be correct, you can actually make a good deal of profit.

In the case of options trading, you will be buying and selling options on large scale futures, stocks, etc. You can invest by determining whether the price will go up or down over a fixed time period. As with trading of Forex, one can easily leverage their power of buying for controlling a greater number of future or stock for instance, that he/she could have generally. But there are certain differences between options trading and forex which has been described properly below.

24 Hour Trading

An advantage that you can get with forex trading when compared to options trading is that you will be having the capability of trading for 24 hours in a day and five days in a week if you feel like. The market of forex is generally open for a longer period of time than any other trading market. If your target is to make profits in double digits in the market, it is actually a great thing when you have an unlimited amount of time every week for making all those trades. Whenever any form of big event takes place anywhere in the world, you can turn out to be the first individual in taking full advantage of that very situation with the trading of forex. You are not required to wait for a long time for the market to open during the morning as you would have to do in case of options trading. You have the power of trading directly from your PC, each and every hour of the day.

Rapid Execution of Trade

With the trading system of forex, you can receive immediate executions of trade. You will be facing no form of delay which is in the case of options trading or for other forms of the market as well. Your order will get filled at the price that is best possible in place of just guessing the price in which you should fill up the order. The order of your choice will not just slip which can happen with options trading. In forex trading, the rate of liquidity is a lot more for helping with the slippage which is present in trading of options.

No Commissions

FX trading or forex trading is generally free from any form of commission. It is mainly because, in forex trading, everything takes place between banks that also match the buyers with the potential sellers and that too super quick. So, in short, in forex trading, the market is inter-bank. Thus, there are no signs of brokerage fees or middleman fees which is the case with the other sort of markets. There is a huge spread between the asking price and the bid. This is where the firms of forex trading tend to make some of their profits. In options trading, you are required to pay out brokerage fees, whether you want to buy or sell. So, you can save a lot of money if you trade in forex markets when compared to the markets of options trading as there are no commissions.

Greater Leverage

In forex trading, you can get greater leverage when compared to options trading. But, with options trading, you will also be able to manage calls and put options in a way for greatly increasing the leverage. Leverage might turn out to be very important when you actually know what is going to be done by a currency. It is possible to achieve 200:1 or even greater in forex trading when compared to options trading, but it can also reach close. So, it can be said that with forex trading, one can make more profit if the right move is made.

Limited Nature of Risk Is Guaranteed

As the traders of forex need to have limits of position, the risk associated with it is also limited as the capabilities of the online system of forex trading can automatically start a margin call when the amount of margin turns out to be much greater than the account value in dollars. This helps the traders of forex from losing not so much if by chance their very own position tends to go the other way. It is actually a great feature of safety which is not available all the time in other markets of financing. How are options different from forex in this aspect? In the options aspect, you can only have a limited amount of time for trading right before the expiration of the options.

Higher Variability

In forex trading markets, the rate of variability is much higher and thus it can result in more risk for the traders. In the markets of forex, the traders are required to decide the direction in which their assets will be going and also have to predict low or high the assets will go. So, it can be stated that the ultimate profit and risk are completely unknown. In forex trading, there are actually no barriers to the amount of money that the traders can lose or make, until and unless they start using certain tools for controlling their trading. One of such tools is a stop loss, which helps in preventing the traders from not losing more than a specific amount of money. In simple terms, once the related trader has already lost a certain amount of money, the trade will be closed automatically. The maximum loss that someone can have in forex trading is all the money that they have in their account of trading.

This is not the case with options trading. It is all about the strike price and expiry time where the traders lose only a certain amount of money, nothing big.

While considering the primary differences between options trading and forex trading, always remember your very own style of trading and the risk type that you will actually be able to handle. There are obvious advantages in forex trading as well as in options trading that can permit you to gain a good amount of profit. But this can only be achieved if you can develop a system that is actually functional and that can stay within the limits of your trading. So, for becoming a really successful trader, you first need to properly learn the major differences between the two markets of trading.

Stocks and Options

If you really want to be a successful investor, you will need to have a proper understanding of the various opportunities of investment first. Most people allow their advisors of investment to take the decisions instead of them. While talking about opportunities of investing, options and stocks are two of the most common markets of investment. It is true that both are traded in a similar way, but there still lies some difference between the two. Stock is an instrument of financing. It shows up ownership of a business and it also helps in signifying a proper claim on the business profits and assets. In simple terms, when you have the stocks of a certain company, you actually own a part of it which is proportional to the total share numbers that the company has. For instance, when you own about 100 shares of a company that has in total 1000 shares, you actually own 10% of that company.

Well, as you already know, options are the contracts of selling or buying an asset, at a fixed price and within a fixed time. Unlike the case of stocks, the contracts of options will not provide you with direct ownership of any company, but it will permit you with the right of selling and buying a great number of the stocks of the company.

Leveraged Profits

The holders of options contracts can take full advantage of the leveraged nature of profits. For instance, when the price of any stock rises by one percent, the price of the options is most likely to rise by ten percent. So, it can be stated that the profits of options are ten times more than the stock price in this case.

Downside Earning of Profits

For earning profit from the decline in the prices of a stock, the traders can easily short the instruments of financing. This generally results in going through the unlimited nature of losses along with margins if, by chance, the stock price tends to rise again. A trader can only short any stock with the given margin that is enabled with the accounts of trading. On the other hand, if you choose to trade options, you will be able to earn profits even from the decline of prices of the underlying assets by simply purchasing a put option. The value of the put options tends to rise as the overall value of the underlying assets tends to decrease. So, any holder of options can easily take full advantage of the reduction in prices as well. As you buy any put options, you are not required to pay any kind of margin. The losses will be limited only up to the value of the option that was previously paid for buying all the securities.

Limitation of Time

Options come with a limited time frame. Thus, options can be held by any holder of option only till the expiration time. But, in the case of stocks, if the user opts for a short or long position, he/she can keep the stock for an indefinite frame of time.

Movement of Price

When there is variation in the overall price of any stock, the price of the options will also tend to vary. But, the value variation of the options is comparatively low. The extent of how close the variation of price of the options matches along with the variation of stock variation can be calculated by the strike price which is generally defined in the contract of options.

Worthless Expiry

The primary reason why a majority of the people who are holders of options end up in losing their entire investments in a short period of time is mainly because all these derivatives tend to end up with a worthless nature of expiry in case the underlying assets fail to perform in the way as expected within a fixed time frame. That is the reason why the trading of all these instruments of finance is considered as a high profit-high risk activity. But, if you end up buying stocks, you have the power of keeping all the underlying securities within your portfolio as long as you want them to if the price of the same does not tend to rise up. It is possible to easily benefit from the rise in the price of stocks even if it actually takes several years to happen.

Price

In this world, everyone is trying to save money. In that case, options are much cheaper when compared to stocks. But, in the case of stocks, they are actually very expensive. Each contract of an option can gives you overall control of about 100 shares of equity, but still, the cost that is needed for purchasing contracts of options is actually far away from the expense of buying an equal amount of stock.

CHAPTER 16:

Money Management

Investing can seem incredibly difficult. You might get intimidated when you start investing. There is also the choice to choose from thousands of shares and at least as many funds. And then you still have to determine when it is time to buy and sell. For beginners, the stock market can seem incredibly lucrative, risky, and confusing. Some basic lessons about the stock market can already save you from the most common mistakes and pitfalls. This way, you remain motivated to learn more about investing and investing.

Do you find it difficult? Or maybe there is a simple strategy that can help starters on their way. Who wants to invest successfully keeps it simple. Follow those simplified guides as you start your investing adventure. It could mark the beginning of something truly amazing in your life. The only thing that separates successful investors from failures is the amount of actionable step they took on the valuable information that's available to them.

Start with a diversified basis

Leonardi Da Vinci stated in the famed Wolf of Wall Street movie: "Simplicity is the ultimate sophistication." A good portfolio excels in a good diversification strategy. A portfolio does not have to contain 30 items, but a correctly balanced mix that keeps risk and returns in balance. Or, as John Templeton said: "Diversify. In stocks and bonds, as in much else, there is safety in numbers." There is plenty of options: from gold, over ETFs, to real estate, currencies, index funds or shares. Create a clear portfolio where you, as an investor, know how to deal with the risk.

Build in a buffer for yourself

Investing is never without risk. The risk-free investment does not pay off; it only costs money. To avoid jeopardizing your healthy financial situation, put some money aside in advance. We usually assume that six months of fixed costs is enough to bridge worse times. If there are indispensable opportunities in the financial markets, you can still use part of this capital to participate. Do estimate whether these opportunities are worth your buffer.

Search for the adventure and discover

If there is still some financial breathing room, you can still look for the adventure. A more aggressive investment means more risk but also a potentially greater return. Again, you can limit the risk here by diversifying. As they say about the channel: "Don't put all your eggs in one basket."

Limit losses and cash your winnings

Every investor experience it sometimes. You have a fantastic share in your portfolio, and week after week, it performs better. And suddenly there is a turning point, you have hope for recovery, but the decline continues. Until it gets to a phase where you get to make decisions. If you are not prepared to undergo such a rollercoaster, then be wise. Is your investment doubling? Then sell half and secure your investment. When you purchase a share, you can work with a stop-loss order. A percentage of 20 percent is common.

This means an automatic sale when the acceptable limit of loss has been exceeded. It limits your loss and allows you to reinvest with your new capital in what will hopefully become a more successful business. A perfect strategy does not exist because you may have to grind and watch how the stock wins again after the sale. A strategy that helps to start investors to keep their night's sleep.

View the total financial picture

Making a profit on an investment is quite a pleasant feeling. But investments are not alone, not on an island, or floating in a vacuum. Investments are part of your total financial life. Many asset managers give their clients wise advice: you have to manage your accounting as a business.

That may mean that you have to monitor your debt ratio properly. For example, some investors try to counter a lesser investment with a more robust (and often riskier) investment in the hope of making up for one misconception with an absolute jackpot. With that, they naturally run even more risk while this wasn't necessary—a sad side effect for someone who loses sight of his total accounting. Slowly trying to solve the debts of that misconception and at the same time, creating an emergency fund would certainly be a more solid approach to the problem. In this way, you create a sustainable solution, and you learn from a mistake while correcting it. It is especially important to have a sound financial basis before you venture into the stock market. Every other aspect of that personal financial accounting must be perfect.

Feel comfortable with your investment

Many people who invest and invest today grew up in a different spirit of the times. Thirty years ago, it was fashionable to get as much return as possible. Thanks to the internet, the declining pensions and changes in the banking landscape, a lot has changed over time. Modern investing and investing are mainly focused on risk and no longer on returns. Most people who invest because of a supplementary pension are focused on avoiding losses instead of making big profits. So, their hope is not to become rich or richer per se, but to have enough capital in their old age to survive.

The stock market is not a casino

Whoever plays poker knows that "all-in" already dare to pay all. You bet all your money on one game in the hope of surviving or winning the jackpot. Don't count on that opportunity when you talk about the stock market. To go all out on a single stock with all your money is never a good idea. Even the most experienced stock traders diversify their portfolio to minimize losses. In recent times, many interesting IPOs have sprung up. Although the attraction is very high among investors and investors, the lion's share among them is aware that this is not the best choice. Novice investors are often blinded by the atmosphere, the hurray mood, and the influence of others. Therefore, always realize that you do not play with money; you invest it for a specific purpose in mind.

Investing is not a hobby

Don't get us wrong: investing can be incredibly fun, but you cannot view it as a non-binding hobby. Of course, big banks see investing as a very competitive business. That's why it's best to look at your portfolio through the eyes of a professional. It is important to understand your portfolio well, understand where your profit but also loss comes from. You must also be able to understand the companies in which you invest. Once you have completed this entire process, everything becomes so much easier. "Will this investment or investment earn me money, or will I tear it off?" An obvious question is not always asked.

Beginners often invest in stocks that seem attractive to them—a wrong motivation with often the wrong result. In the beginning, investing can sometimes have great similarities with gambling, and many starting investors want to understand how the stock market works. They soon realize the movements of large indexes, but the real work only starts when they take the investment fully seriously. Benjamin Graham said it a few decades ago: "You only do smart investment if you look at it as a business." Fund managers, analysts, traders, and other experts in financial centers take stock trading very seriously and so you better take up the challenge.

Financial resources

Before you start investing, you should better inform yourself about economic developments and prospects, the markets, and the shares that interest you. You don't have to look far: read the newspaper every day. Financial newspapers such as De Tijd, Financial Times, Wall Street Journal, can help you keep up with the most important issues. You can also consult financial websites such as Yahoo finance. Professional investors also use accounts on services such as Bloomberg and Reuters. Since everyone learns the same things at the same time, these may not be the places to make the distinction. And yet you should not try to follow in the footsteps of the experts too much. Some of the best-known investors, such as Peter Lynch, suggested that hints from daily life could provide more inspiration.

Form a Strategic Daily spending patterns

For example, Lynch "used" his wife's shopping habits to analyze which brands gained popularity. According to Lynch, traders and stock traders spent too much time in an artificial bubble. Peter Lynch's views are not old-fashioned. In 2012, a financial nitwit put the test to the test and succeeded in suddenly making 2 million dollars during a difficult stock market period of $ 20,000. Everything but a cold trick.

According to the amateur investor, there were clear trends in the spending patterns of women, young people, and low incomes. The man invested in shares that everyone could own and noticed trends before bankers saw them and made substantial gains.

How can you monitor your stock portfolio?

If you decide to invest in shares, drawing up an investment plan is the first step. However, once you have compiled your equity portfolio, you are not yet ready. Monitoring your equity portfolio to monitor whether it still meets your original objectives is just as important. Some investors like to check the status of their investments every day. But for many investors, this is not desirable or necessary. In other words, monitoring your equity portfolio depends on both the type of investments in your portfolio and the type of investor that you are.

Monitor shares

The moment you have invested not in funds, but self-selected individual shares, it is interesting to monitor these continuously. The most important goal here is to check if a share still meets your initial criteria. In almost all cases, this will depend strongly on your estimate of the future expectation for the underlying company or the estimate of the stock market. Many of these estimates are based on company income. You have to monitor the changes that affect income.

Newspapers, press releases, and reports

Check the financial news and announcements about your shares daily, weekly, or monthly. This includes new products, changes in management, or news about competitors. If analysts report on your share, it is wise always to read it immediately. Since these can be of great importance for market sentiment.

Online sources of news

Many brokers allow you to monitor your stock portfolio online. In some cases, there is even a direct link to news and analysis of the relevant share. This way, you not only see at a glance how your portfolio is doing, but you also have an overview of relevant news sources that can influence the price. Many brokers also offer the option to receive alerts by e-mail or text message when certain developments occur on the market. Does your broker not have such an option? Then online portals like finance. yahoos allow you to enter your portfolio. After which they will provide you with a large number of relevant news sources. Both through your broker and financial websites such as Yahoo Finance, Morningstar, and Bloomberg, you will be provided with information in real-time. Since the stock market also responds to developments in real-time, this information can enable you to react promptly to developments to maximize your returns.

Follow up your portfolio mobile

Although many professional traders still have an old-fashioned Bloomberg terminal in the office, there is an easier way. Some many mobile sites and apps provide you with the same information, but at the same time also fit in your pocket. For example, newspapers such as De Standard, De Tijd have their apps, but you can also find everything with Bloomberg Markets +, Yahoo Finance, and Google Finance. Most major brokers also have mobile applications available, with which you cannot find information, but can also easily invest in mobile.

CHAPTER 17:

Tactics for Success

Which Trading Is Profitable?

There are several basic kinds of options trading activities that the novice and even the experienced traders should be familiar with and get to master their favorite kinds of options trading that it is much going to be profitable during various occurrences. Here are some of the profitable ways.

Buy to open. This involves initiating a new order to secure a new option and eventually getting to improve on the existing trading position as judged from the past trading activities.

Sell to open. Selling to open is selling a specific option that you do not necessarily own and in the end, acquiring a new position or an improved position in the options trading activities.

Buying to close. This is buying a specific option that you had previously sold in the market and eventually reducing a position in the options trading market.

Selling to close. In this kind of trading, an order to sell a specific option is exercised, where whatever you are selling had been previously been bought and end up reducing or exiting an existing position in the trading market.

How to Be a Successful Options Trader

Below are some of the ways we can shine on this options trading field.

Risk management. Life is a risk itself, implying that risks will always be depicted. An options trader needs to master all the possible ways in which he or she can minimize the number of risks that are likely to occur and learn from everyone of it for future good management. For instance, in the capital sector, the trader ought to have a big plan entailing details on how capital should be used strictly. Losses are also part of the options trading aftermath, and with bad capital handle, everything can tumble down. Think of how bad the market volatility can stand, leading to a great amount of capital, and leading to large chunks of losses.

Be the chief in numbers. Options trading involves wide use of numbers. Do you know the implied volatility? Is money in the option or out of the option? For beginners who have no single trace of what is going on, kindly commit oneself to some in-depth research and try to get a spotlight. For the intermediate and experts, keep learning about various numbers in options trading. Life stops once you stop learning.

Possess great discipline. Self-discipline is encouraged as you get involved in options trading. This is the up-thrust motive force that will drive you towards as per your agenda plans with so much determination. You get to follow your specific laid plans and strategies, learn so much from your trading activities, and get the respective skills and experience for more successful options trading. Remember that your set plan strategies are the core objects during options trading, implying that self-discipline will bring you nothing but great success.

Great patience. Every aspect of life is a process led by constant growth. Trade during several market movements and get to learn from it. During this options trading journey, you will be exposed to various occurrences that you need to learn and master each one of them. Learn the possible risks involved, several market tricks and so much on. Well, get the best experience for it is always the best tutor.

Have your trading style. The intended trading style is what's normally implemented in the trading plan. Your trading style should be strictly adhered to and updated with new skills and information as you get involved in various options trading activities. Follow your plan without any other kind of influence and watch yourself grow with options trading.

A trading plans. Failing to plan is planning to fail. This implies that failing will only be reflected once planning does not happen. Successful options traders have big plans. Big plans entail good laid strategies, functions, discussions, in-depth research, great self-discipline, targets, and good goals. Establishing good trading plans is a clear reflection of great success in options trading.

Emotionally stable. Emotions can be quite a distraction as we get involved in different aspects of our lives. Losing a trade should be viewed just like a bad day that comes in handy with a good learning experience and knowledge for a bright future. Winning days should also be a learning day by valuing the good moves expressed that day.

Intensive learning and being proactive. Life always remains stagnant when you stop learning. Learning is achieved from the good side and the bad side, in that, master and learn every possible move expressed in options trading and be quite interested in picking the essence morals from the past episodes and squeezing any goodness from it. Also, subscribe to various well-contented channels and blogs to get the wide knowledge that is needed in options trading. Learning makes you informed and educated on the actual trade activities that are commonly involved in options trading.

Secure, accurate trading records. Try to learn from your mistakes though it can be tricky at times to formulate straight decisions based on your past performance since options trading is a matter of happy and sad seasons governed by several set strategies that have been correctly laid in the options trading plan. It is encouraged to learn from your past mistakes and get to grow strategically to become a successful options trader.

Determination and commitment. This entails the high thrust force that should govern a beginner or any kind of experienced trader to acquire what is best for him or her in options trading and getting to know the several tips on becoming a successful options trader.

Be flexible. Another point to add is that when you feel that the market does not suit you at all that particular options trading period, find something constructive to do. Master any possible market move that is likely to take place in options trading and master it.

Basic understanding and interpretation. The trader should familiarize himself or herself with the basic market terminologies to understand the basic activities of the market and get to know the various ways on how to begin and handle option trading. Interpretation involves getting to analyze the actual options trading happenings in the market and sourcing the essentials in every trading activity. This helps the trader to always look out for the reality of the market rather than the hype and depending on the major market deadlines.

Be aggressive. Being aggressive in options trading essentially implies that there is a thirst for great success, and the chances of acquiring large amounts of profits are so high. An aggressive option trader is mostly partaking in-depth research learning new and learning new lucrative trading moves. This gives the trader much experience and skills to face any kind of risks that are likely to be involved in the market and, within no time, the trader has accredited a great expert in options trading.

Emotionally stable. The trader involved in options trading should not be controlled by various feelings experienced in the market. The losing days should not discourage the trader in any way such that he or she decides to stick with the market hype. It is highly recommended that traders should follow their plan and always stick to their various strategies.

Good stock pick. An options trader needs to pick the right option to sell. Weigh whether you are capable of handling the respective stock and managing the necessary risks highly involved in it. Most importantly, is the stock going to benefit the trader from acquiring large amounts of profits?

Good capital management. Money is really important when it comes to trading. Monitor and plan for every amount of capital you plan to utilize in the market. Always be careful in the amount of money you place in every option. Acquiring losses is always an alternative when it comes to option trading, a breakdown that can tumble you so badly and make you bankrupt as well. Plan for the capital you plan to invest in the company.

Powerful trading platforms. The kind of platform where various trading activities are taking place is pretty much important in any kind of options trading involvement. Your best platform should consist of awesome navigation tools, learning sources, and other amazing features.

Selling options. Selling options is mostly preferred rather than buying options while practicing the call and put strategies that eventually help the trader to gain a good amount of profits.

Correct timing. As a trader, you should be informed of the good times and the bad times. Enter the market when the timing is quite favorable. Bad timing leads to great amounts of losses being made at the options trading market leading to a great downfall of finances. Bad timing leads to great amounts of losses being made at the options trading market leading to a great downfall of finances that, after all, causes bankruptcy.

Strategies to Be Successful in Options Trading

Good strategies set in the options trading plan should be prioritized. Backtesting, measuring and weighing the current laid strategies by comparing them with some former historical records and learning the growth and the happenings that have happened in the recent periods, is highly recommended by the expert traders. Major strategies are going to be tackled later on in the book but meanwhile, let us peep at some of the strategies that should be considered:

Use a proper time period. A longer period, for instance, five years, is recommended during in-depth research and during analyzing the various sources to lay some good strategies. Remember to pick a quite long period to get the actual information and report in all that as part of learning.

Covered call. This kind of strategy involves both trading on the underlying stock and also to those of the options contract. The end goal of a covered call is to collect income through the premiums and majorly selling the stock amount that you already possess. Below are some the ways you need to consider in creating a covered call:

Purchase a stock and buy it in the form of shares.

For every 100 shares you own, sell a call contract.

Then hold on for the call to be exercised.

The kind of risk involved in covered calls holds the stock position carefully that could fail with time. The large chunks of profits of this particular call are equal to the price of a specific call option and a lower purchase price of the underlying stock.

Market put. This strategy involves the trader had made two purchases of stock trading and that of a put option. The benefit of this is that you, as an options trader, can shield oneself from several losses' occurrences. The market put is also considered advantageous during purchasing a security that is bearing a bullish outlook. The market put strategy is also essential when protecting depreciation in particular stock prices.

The market put is also referred to as a synthetic long call due to the similarities in the number of profit potentials on both sides.

Options spread. This strategy is established by selling several options and purchasing options of the same class and from the same security with various strike prices and expiration dates.

Butterfly spread. Butterfly involves four calls and puts and also considered as a market-neutral strategy that gets to pay most of its underlying stock without the concern of the expiration dates involved.

There are several varieties of butterfly spreads that normally use four kinds of options with three different strike prices. To add, different kinds of butterfly have different levels of the maximum profit amount and the maximum loss amount that are normally experienced during options trading.

Short bull ratio strategy. Short bull ratio strategy is used to benefit from the amounts of profits gained from increasing security involved in the trading market in a similar way in which we normally get to buy calls during a particular period.

CHAPTER 18:

Binary Options

This is similar to traditional options in many ways except that they ultimately boil down to a basic yes or no question. Instead of worrying about what exact price an underlying stock is going to have, it only cares if it is going to be above one price at the time of its expiration. Traders then make their exchange if they think that the answer is just a yes or a no. While it may seem simple on its face, it is important that you carefully understood how binary options work, as well as the time frames and markets they work with. It is also important to understand the specific criteria that they have and what legal companies are allowed to offer binary options for trade.

If you are currently considering trading in binary options, then it is also important to be aware that binary options trading outside of the US has a different structure. Also, when hedging or speculating, it is important to keep in mind that doing so is considered an exotic options trade, so the rules are different still. Regardless, the price of a binary options is always going to be somewhere between $0 and $100, it is also going to come with a bid price as well as an ask price, just like any other type of option.

They are also a great way for those who are interested in day-trading but do not have the serious capital required to get off the ground, to ply their trade. Traditional stock day trading limits do not apply to binary options, so you are allowed to start trading with just 1, $100 deposit. It is also important to keep in mind that binary options are a derivative created by its association with an underlying asset which means they do not give you ownership of that asset in any way. This means you cannot exercise them to generate dividends or enact voting rights as you would with standard options.

For example, assume you are considering purchasing a binary option that states that the gold's price will be greater than $1,250 by $1:30 pm. If you have faith in the scenario is going to come true, then you would want to buy into the option. Otherwise, you would want to sell it. Further assume that the option is trading at a bid price of $42.50 and an ask price of $44.50, 30 minutes before it is set to expire. If you opt to buy the binary option at this point, you have to pay $44.50. Otherwise, you would pay $42.50 to sell it.

If you buy in at $44.50 and then by 1:30 the gold's price is North of 1,250, then your option would expire successfully and has reached its max which is $100. You garnered a profit of $55.50 before fees are taken into account. But when the price ends up lower than $1,250, then the option becomes worth $0, and you lose out on your $44.50. The offer and bid prices are going to continue to oscillate until it has to expire, but you have the opportunity to close your position whenever you like, just as with other types of options.

Sooner or later, every option is either going to be worth $100 or be worth $0. The bid price and the ask price are set as the traders who are considering the trade determine the likelihood of success. The higher the bid and ask price are, the greater the overall perceived likelihood of the option coming true. If they are near 50, then the odds are average, and if they are very low then they are not skewed in favor of the average at all.

Where to trade binary options: Binary options are now traded on the Nadex exchange, the original exchange dedicated to legally selling binary options in the US. It offers browser-based trading via its own platform which offers real-time charts as well as market access to the latest binary options prices.

Binary options can also be traded via the Chicago Board Options Exchange (CBOE). It can be accessed with a brokerage account that is approved for options trading via their standard access routes. It is important to keep in mind, however, that not all brokers are equipped to offer options trading. As such, before you get started trading in options it is important that you make sure your broker offers all the trading possibilities that you may one day consider as changing horses mid-stream can be quite complicated.

Trading on the Nadex costs 90 cents when entering a trade and the same when exiting from one. The fee is capped at $9 per trade so purchasing a lot of 15 will still only cost $9. If you hold your trade until it expires then the fees will be taken out at that point. If the trade ends up being out of the money when it expires you will not be charged a fee. Trading via CBOE is handled through specific options brokers who charge a variety of different commission fees.

Choosing a binary market: You are free to trade in multiple classes of assets with binary options. Nadex allows for trading in all of the major indices including the Dow 30, Russell 2000, the Nasdaq 100 and the S&P 500. Global indices including those from Japan, Germany, and the UK are also available. Trades are also available for a variety of forex pairs including AUD/JPY, EUR/GBP, USD/CHF, GBP/JPY, USD/CAD, AUD/USD, EUR/JPY, USD/JPY, GBP/UDS AND EUR/USD.

Additionally, Nadex also offers trading in commodity binary options including soybeans, corn, copper, silver, gold, natural gas and crude oil. You are also provided with the option to trading based on specific news events. You can buy options based on whether the Federal Reserve is going to decrease or increase the rates of things like joblessness claims or whether or not the number of nonfarm payrolls is going to beat its estimates or not.

The BVOE offers a smaller variance of binary options to choose from that are not currently available anywhere else. There you can buy binary options based on their own interpretation of the current state of the S&P 500 and a volatility option index based on its own volatility index.

Risk and reward: Binary option risk is capped at the cost of the initial trade as the worst thing that will ever happen is that your option expires at 0. The risk is also capped, though it can still offer up significant returns depending on the amount of the initial investment. For example, if you purchase a binary option for $20, that ends up paying out, then you will still make $100 off of it ($80 profit) which means you have a 4:1 reward ratio which is more than you could find if you invested in the related stock directly.

This only works out in your favor to a point, however, as your gains will always top out at $100, no matter how much movement the underlying stock actually experienced. This downside can be mitigated to some extent simply by purchasing multiple options contracts up front.

Binary Option Strategies

Pinocchio strategy: This is the perfect strategy to put into play if you come across a candle bar with an extremely long wick and a very small body during the course of your technical analysis. This type of bar is known as a pin bar, but it was given its more descriptive name because the longer the wick grows, the more likely it is to be giving you false information.

If you come across this scenario and the wick is already quite long, then you can generally assume that the price of the underlying stock will have moved about as far as it can in the current direction and that it will likely be reversing quite soon. As such, when you see this bar then you will know that your best bet is to start trading against the majority as the trend is likely going to turn and benefit your new position. After the wick begins shrinking, you will then want to generate a prediction on a call, and if it begins to increase again, then you will want to change your prediction to a put.

Binary option reversal strategy: The effectiveness of this strategy is because the market naturally seeks balance which means that any price is bound to turn around eventually when confronted with extreme highs or lows. As such, when it comes to binary options, you can get a jump on the movement by predicting what is likely going to happen next.

For this strategy to work out effectively, you are going to need to predict the need for a put or a call based on the situation as it stands with help from information from external sources. You will find this to be a very useful strategy during periods of rapid asset movement because the speed at which it moves one way will be the same amount of speed with which it will eventually move back the other way. Because asset movement is bound to repeat itself eventually, once you understand its patterns you will be able to naturally tell when a given underlying asset is at its peak, making any relevant binary options a very clear-cut decision.

Martingale strategy: In scenarios where you are more or less unconfident in the current state of the market but still want to keep an eye on a given investment the martingale strategy can be quite useful. This strategy is also different than most other strategies as it involves heavily doubling down due to binary options' unique characteristics. As an example, if you start with a $20 binary option that does not pay out, then your next binary option should be worth $30 on the opposite side and so on and so forth until you make a profit. If your amounts get to the point where a $100 profit would not square you, then you would want to purchase multiple contracts at once.

This strategy is going to appeal to those who are naturally inclined to take risky investments that have a higher overall promise of return as well. With that being said, much of the risk can be minimized if you are familiar with the asset you are purchasing contracts on as you will already know the scope of the market and will not have to rely on the strategy to help you learn the ins and outs through unsuccessful contracts. This strategy is somewhat unique in that its odds of being successful are based almost entirely on your personal level of familiarity with the underlying asset.

Trade the news: Buying into binary options contracts for a variety of assets based on the news is an effective means of working with binary options that is more multifaceted than it may first appear. At its most basic, it involves purchasing contracts when good news is forthcoming and selling them when bad news is on the horizon. Unlike other types of analysis, it is much less of a science which goes in line with the more generalized nature of binary options in general. The most important thing you will need to learn to this type of analysis is how much of an effect a given piece of news is going to have on a specific underlying asset.

CHAPTER 19:

Finding a Broker

W hen it comes to finding the right broker, the cheapest option is not always the best. You will find that spending some time evaluating brokers will guide you to the right choice, one that will give you quality services. With experience, you will also see that a diligent and reliable broker serves better, even if its fees are high compared to a cheap brokerage. Below are some of the factors you ought to consider when trying to find the right brokerage for your options investment needs.

What to Look for in a Broker

Discount Versus Full-Service Broker

Before going any further, you must first know that there are two kinds of brokers in the market: the self-directed discount brokerage and the full-service brokerage.

The self-directed discount brokerage is the type that is built specifically to suit the needs of the self-directed or independent trader. In this case, the brokerage does not offer any investment advice but leaves the clients to make their own financial decisions. These brokerages only execute the clients' orders. For this reason, discount brokerages charge so much less than their full-service counterparts do.

The full-service brokers, the traditional brokers, are brokerages that provide a range of services at a fee. Among other services, these brokers give professional advice to their clients on the best investment opportunities.

☐   Some brokerages offer a combination of full-service and self-directed services. Their services are ranked relative to the help that each investor category needs, and the clients only must choose, depending on the quality of services they need.

Most investors opt for the discount brokerages, and I presume that it is because anyone that gets into options trading must already have been running different investment instruments in the past and are knowledgeable in finance and investment matters, enough not to need a broker's help. They do this particularly when the broker's fee is measured by the number of trades performed rather than on the soundness of the advice a broker provides.

Fees and Commissions

One of the edges of competition for brokers is the cost of their services. Brokerages come up with creative ways to make money out of the activities of the traders, and you need to carefully examine the charges imposed before you settle for any single brokerage. Look at the contract fee and the per-trade fee.

The per-contract fee is the fee charged for every option contract signed in each trade, while the per trade is the minimum fee charged per transaction regardless of the number of contracts involved in each trade.

☐ The total commission costs for each transaction is calculated using the following formula:

☐ Total Commission = $X for each trade + $Y per contract

Here's another formula brokerage has taken up:

Total Commission = Whichever is higher ($X for each trade or $Y for each contract)

Volume Discount

Some brokerages offer discounts by charging a lower fee for a trading frequency that goes beyond a threshold. Therefore, if you plan to make numerous trades within the month, it makes sense to scout for a brokerage firm that has this discount scheme.

Limit or Market Order

Some brokerages have differentiated fees for different kinds of orders; ensure that you take note of the charges for limit orders. Traders rarely make market orders.

Broker-Assisted vs. Internet Trading

If you choose to trade with the help or guidance of your broker, it may cost you as much, or several times more than the independent internet trades. Therefore, to save on your costs, only choose broker-assisted trading when you know you will have no access to the internet because then, an excellent opportunity could come up, and you would need to take it up.

Disguised Fees

Some brokerages charge low fees, but they make up for the low rates with some hidden charges. Therefore, if you come across a brokerage that charges unusually low fees in comparison to its competition, ensure that you look around to see whether the brokerage has placed some disguised fees.

Some of the hidden fees you ought to look out for include:

Minimum Balance Fee: This is a periodical fee levied (every month or after every quarter) if your account goes below a set threshold.

Account Inactivity Fee: Is the fee that some brokerages charge if the trader has not made any trade in a period.

Annual Maintenance Fee: Is the fee that brokerages charge every year you hold an account with them, whether you have been making trades or not.

It is crucial that you give careful consideration to   the commissions and fees charged because they have   a significant impact on the profits or the losses yo u make, especially if your trading capital places a cap on   the   number of contracts you can make for each trade. For example, some brokers limit you to only having 1 or 2 contracts for each trade while others set the win/loss ratio to 6:4, or less. You need to know that a low-commissions broker is important because it can boost your earnings by up to 50%.

Quality of Service

While making consideration of the fees and commissions charged affects the profitability of your trading, this ought not to be the only consideration. Other factors such as the ease of use, execution speed, and site availability matter, particularly in the case of self-directed online trading, also determine the quality of services a broker provides.

Here's a brief description of why you should consider each of the factors mentioned above.

Ease of Use

By themselves, options are already a complicated lot, and using a complicated platform or brokerage would only make things worse. However, an easy-to-use interface helps to make your activities smoother and to minimize errors. If the interface is not right, trading mistakes that would follow will cause the loss of large sums of money because money in the options market changes hands every day. Therefore, when looking for a trading platform, opt for one that offers all its resources on a single screen for easy access.

Quality of Execution

The SEC, through the National Best Bid or Offer (NBBO), requires brokers to offer the customers the finest obtainable asking price in the market when they buy securities and the finest possible proposal price to traders seeking to sell securities. Ensure that your broker guarantees trade execution prices that meet or even exceed the SEC requirements.

Availability and Speed of Execution

Perhaps the most important factors to consider when selecting a brokerage are the availability of the site and its responsiveness. Options trading is time-sensitive, and you need to execute your trades immediately an opportunity comes up. However low the commission, and the fees are, if you cannot make the trades, or the site takes too long to load and execute commands, taking up this site will only cause you to waste your resources. The amount you save in commissions and fees will not be worth it.

A responsive site ensures that your price quotes are timely. In this information age, information moves fast, across the globe, day, and night. As such, traders should be able to react to breaking news very fast. You will not want to be the trader that lags and only hears of opportunities when other traders have taken them up.

Kindly note that the speed of your internet determines the speed of execution. Therefore, ensure that you take up a package that guarantees speed. A broadband connection is faster than dialup. Before you get on to the brokerage site, ensure that your connectivity is good.

Free Education

If you are a newbie or a seasoned trader that wants to expand his knowledge of options trading strategies, education should be at the forefront of your considerations for possible brokerages. You must get a broker that offers educational resources in the form of live or recorded webinars, online options trading courses, face-to-face meetings with a mentor, and one-on-one guidance via phone or through online means.

You see, options trading is complex, and you may want to spend the first few months, or even years, on the student- teacher learning mode. Get as much education and training as you can. If you come across a broker who offers a simulated, virtual, trial version of the options trading platform, take up the opportunity and test-drive with the dummy account before you can place any real money on the line.

Quality of Customer Service

Customer service matters greatly. You wouldn't want to be stuck with a broker that does not respond to you, or if you make a request or inquiry, the broker responds days or weeks later. Reliable customer service is a priority item, especially for those that are new to options trading. Experienced traders conducting complex trades also need all the help they can get.

As you choose between brokers, think of the means of communication you would wish to have with the broker. Would you like to speak with them on the phone, via email or to meet them in person for a live chat? Is the trading desk on call during the stipulated hours? If you are not sure of this, make several test calls to potential brokers to gauge their availability and responsiveness. Are they available 24 hours 7 days a week, or are they only available during the week? Are the representatives with whom you speak knowledgeably about options and options trading?

Before you settle for any trading platform or broker, ensure that you reach out and ask a few critical questions. See the quality of answers you get, and the time it takes to get them. If the answers are satisfactory, having considered other factors, make your choice of brokerage.

CHAPTER 20:

Avoiding Common Pitfalls in Options Trading

All successful options traders go through a learning curve before they start profiting consistently. Some of them put in an all-out effort to learn by spending countless hours reading on the topic or by watching video tutorials. Others learn at a more leisurely pace and once they get a grip of the basics, they lean more towards learning from their own experience. Irrespective of the type of learner you are, one way to cut short that learning curve is by learning from the mistakes of others.

This is a lists out six of the most common mistakes made by inexperienced traders that can be easily avoided.

1. Buying Naked Options without Hedging

This is one of the most fundamental mistakes made by amateur options traders and is also one of the costliest ones that could make them go broke in no time.

Buying naked options means buying options without any protective trades to cover your investment in the event that the underlying security moves against your expectations and hurts your trade.

Here is a typical example:

A trader strongly feels a particular stock will go up in the short term and assumes he can make a huge profit by buying a few call options and therefore goes ahead with the purchase. The trader knows if the underlying stock's price were to rise as expected, the potential upside on the profits would be unlimited, whereas, if it were to go down, the maximum loss would be curtailed to just the amount invested for purchasing the call options.

In theory, the trader's assumption is right, and it may so happen that this one particular trade may pay off. However, in reality, it is equally possible the stock would not move as per expectations or may even fall. If the latter happens, the call options' prices would start falling rapidly and may never recover thereby causing major losses to that trader.

It is almost impossible to predict the short-term movement of a stock accurately every time and the trader who consistently keeps buying naked options hoping to get lucky is far more likely to lose much more than what he/she gains, in the long term.

For a person to make a profit after buying a naked option, the following things should fall in place:

1. The trader should predict the direction of underlying stock's movement correctly.

2. The directional movement of the stock price should be quick enough so that the position can be closed before its gains get overrun by time-decay.

159

3. The rise in the option's premium price should also compensate for any potential drop in implied volatility from the time the option was purchased.

4. The trader should exit the trade at the right time before a reversal of the stock movement happens.

Needless to say, it is impractical to expect everything to fall in place simultaneously always and that is why naked-options traders often end up losing money even when they correctly guess the direction of the underlying stock's movement.

Having said all this, many such traders often think they would fare better the next time after a botched trade and rinse and repeat their actions till they reach a point where they would have lost most of their capital and are forced to quit trading altogether.

My advice to you – never buy naked options (unless it is part of a larger strategy to hedge some position) because it's simply not worth the risk.

Note: While buying naked-options has only finite risk limited to the price of the premium paid, selling of naked-options has unlimited risk and has to be avoided too, unless hedged properly.

2. Underestimating Time-Decay

A second major mistake of inexperienced traders is underestimating time-decay.

Time-decay is your worst enemy if you are an options buyer and you don't get a chance to exit your trade quickly enough.

If you are a call options buyer, you will notice that sometimes even when your underlying stock's price is increasing every day, your call option's price still doesn't rise or even falls. Alternately, if you are a put options buyer, you sometimes notice that your put option's price doesn't increase despite a fall in the price of the underlying stock. Both these situations can be confusing to somebody new to options trading.

The above problems occur when the rate of increase/decrease in the underlying stock's price is just not enough to outstrip the rate at which the option's time-value is eroding every day.

Therefore, any trade strategy deployed by an options trader should ideally have a method of countering/minimising the effect of time-decay or should make time-decay work in its favour, to ensure a profitable trade.

The spread based strategies do exactly that.

3. Buying Options with High Implied Volatility

Buying options in times of high volatility is yet another common mistake.

During times of high volatility, option premiums can get ridiculously overpriced and at such times, if an options trader buys options, even if the stock moves sharply in line with the trader's expectation, a large drop in the implied volatility would result in the option prices falling by a fair amount, resulting in losses to the buyer.

161

A particular situation I remember happened the day the results of the 'Brexit' referendum came through in 2016. The Nifty index reacting to the result (like most other global indices such as the Nasdaq 100) fell very sharply and the volatility index (VIX) jumped up by over 30%. The options premium for all Nifty options had become ludicrously high that day. However, this rise in volatility was only because of the market's knee-jerk reaction to an unexpected result and just a couple of days later, the market stabilised and started rising again; the VIX fell sharply and also brought down option premium prices accordingly.

Option traders who bought options at the time VIX was high would have realised their mistake a day or two later when the option prices came down causing them substantial losses because the volatility started to get back to normal figures.

4. Not Cutting Losses on Time

There is apparently a famous saying among the folks on Wall Street - "Cut your losses short and let your winners run".

Even the most experienced options traders will make a bad trade once in a while. However, what differentiates them from a novice is that they know when to concede defeat and cut their losses. Amateurs hold on to losing trades in the hope they'll bounce back and eventually end up losing a larger chunk of their capital. The experienced traders, who know when to concede defeat, pull out early, and re-invest the capital elsewhere.

Cutting losses in time is crucial especially when you trade a directional strategy and make a wrong call. The practical thing to do is to exit a losing position if it moves against expectation and erodes more than 2-3% of your total capital.

If you are a trader who strictly uses spread-based strategies, your losses will always be far more limited whenever you make a wrong call. Nevertheless, irrespective of the strategy used, when it becomes evident that the probability of profiting from a trade is too less for whatsoever reason, it is prudent to cut losses and reinvest in a different position that has a greater chance of success rather than simply crossing your fingers or appealing to a higher power.

5. Keeping too many eggs in the same Basket

The experienced hands always know that once in a while, they will lose a trade. They also know that they should never bet too much on a single trade which could considerably erode their capital were it to go wrong.

Professionals spread their risk across different trades and keep a maximum exposure of not more than 4-5% of their total available capital in a single trade for this very reason.

Therefore, if you have a total capital of $10,000, do not enter any single trade that has a risk of losing more than $500 in the worst-case scenario. Following such a practice will ensure the occasional loss is something you can absorb without seriously eroding your cash reserve. Fail to follow this rule and you may have the misfortune of seeing many months of profits wiped out by one losing trade.

6. Using Brokers who charge High Brokerages

A penny saved is a penny earned!

When I first entered the stock market many years ago, I didn't pay much attention to the brokerage I was paying. After all, the trading services I received were from one of the largest and most reputed banks in the country and the brokerage charged by my provider wasn't very different from that of other banks that provided similar services.

Over the years, many discount brokerage firms started flourishing that charged considerably less, but I had not bothered changing my broker since I was used to the old one.

It was only when I quantified the differences that I realised having a low-cost broker made a huge difference.

If you are somebody who trades in the Indian Stock markets, check the table below for a quantified break-up of how brokerage charges can eat into your earnings over a year if you choose the wrong broker. The regular broker in the table below is the bank whose trading services I had been previously using and the discount broker is the one I use now. For the record, the former is also India's third largest bank in the private sector and the latter is the most respected discount broker house in the country.

	Regular Broker	Discount Broker
Brokerage charged per options trade	₹ 300	₹ 20
Cost of entering any directional spread and exiting the position before expiry	₹ 1,200	₹ 80
Cost of entering an Iron Condor and taking it to expiry	₹ 1,200	₹ 80
Percentage of profits surrendered as brokerage for a typical Iron-Condor on Nifty index (Considering profit of ₹ 3300 for a trade with 70% winning probability)	36.36%	2.42%

Comparison of brokerages : Regular Broker versus Discount Broker

It is obvious from the table above that using a low-cost broker makes a huge difference especially when trading a strategy such as the Iron Condor (a relatively low-yield but high-probability strategy).

Also, it is not just the brokerage that burns a hole in your pocket; the annual maintenance fee is also higher for a regular broker and all these costs will make a huge difference in the long run.

Irrespective of which part of the world you trade from, always opt for a broker that provides the lowest possible brokerage because this will make a difference in the long term. Do a quantitative comparison using a table (something similar to the one I used above) and that would make it easier to decide who you should go with.

Note for India-based Traders: If you are a trader based in India or if you trade in the Indian Stock markets, I would strongly suggest using Zerodha, which has been consistently rated the best discount broker in the country. I have been using their services for the past couple of years and have found them to be particularly good. Their brokerage rates are among the best in the country, and on top of that, they provide excellent support when needed, and also maintain an exhaustive knowledgebase of articles. Lastly their trading portal is very user friendly and therefore, placing an order is quick and hassle-free.

To start a trading account with Zerodha, click *here.

*This is an affiliate link. This means that if you open an account using this link, I may be paid a minor commission, though rest assured it won't cost you anything extra. As an author, I don't make much in the way of royalties, so the affiliate commissions would be a welcome bonus to help pay the bills. Lastly, I endorse this service because I use it myself too and have found this service to be extremely satisfactory.

CHAPTER 21:

Trader Psychology

In order to be a successful trader, you need to have a trader mindset. It's important to be disciplined as a trader so that you can avoid the pitfalls that suck in novice traders and lead them to large losses.

Don't Let Emotion Rule Your Trades

One of the problems that happen with trading is that emotions can get intense when there are the possibilities of losing or earning a great deal of money over a short time period. This problem also impacts long term investors, who may become fearful of losing their money when they see stock prices collapsing.

In either case, we are talking about people ruling their investments or trades using emotion instead of the logic that is really needed to make good decisions. For traders, you can help get around this by automating your trades, at least to mitigate downside risk. That way you decide ahead of time what the amount of loss you are willing to accept on the trade is, hopefully by using the 2% rule. That rule has been arrived at by financial experts as a result of analyzing large numbers of trades and determining what a safe level of loss is that you can take on a single trade and largely keep your overall brokerage account relatively intact. That way, you are going to be able to live to trade another day, so to speak.

Long term investors often don't have this kind of protection. The reason is that you don't want to be placing stop-loss orders on long term investments, you are hoping to stay in these investments for the long term, after all. And that means that you are going to need to ride out drops in the stock market without panic. But all too often, long term investors – or people that think of themselves as long term investors, give in to the panic and join the other lemmings running off the cliff and they sell their shares. As we've said repeatedly, this is not something that you want to let yourself do. But, since there is no stop-loss order, you can place to prevent it, you are going to have to seek out discipline and avoid doing it using your own mental effort. This can be difficult during a major crash when you are going to see yourself losing a lot of money on paper. Remember that downtrends are buying opportunities, and so you should be buying up stocks instead of selling them. It's often best to go against the crowd in the stock market, especially when we are talking about small investors.

Traders also need to avoid getting sucked in by greed. In most cases, swing traders are looking at the possibility of making profits from relatively small price movements, and if the price moves to the point at which they need to take profits, but they don't, it can drop 50 cents a share or a dollar a share, and the trader might see the opportunity for profit evaporate. You don't want to hold on too long for profits in a trade, but many traders get overcome by greed and think if they just hold on a little bit longer, they can make big money.

Plan Ahead

This brings us to the next important trader mindset, which is planning. A trader, whether you are a long term investor or some kind of trader like a swing trader, needs to have carefully thought out plans in place that they can use in order to direct their actions when they actually enter a position.

Before entering a trade, a swing trader needs to have the stop loss value for the shares and the take profit value already figured out before you actually buy your shares. A trader who is not planning, and executing specific plans are just groping around in the dark. Instead of doing that you should know beforehand what your goals are, and how you are going to reach your goals. You need to have specific ideas as to how much money you are going to make and how much you are hoping to make every week.

Have a trading routine

It's a good idea to have a trading routine. If you are trading full-time, then you want to have a morning routine that you use to start your trading day. This should include paying attention to financial news so that you can get wind of unexpected results that could impact your trades. Sometimes, there are going to be surprised, that means you might need to change your trading plans.

If you are only trading on a part-time basis, then you should still have a routine that you use daily to stay on top of your trades. Maybe you will do this in part on your lunch hour during workdays so that you can make sure that you are keeping up with the progress of your trades and you have the ability to make some adjustments. In addition, you should also have some time either in the early morning hours, or in the evening, or even both if you are able to, where you analyze your trades or study in order to find new trades to enter.

The specifics of your routine are less important than the fact that you either have one, or you don't. Those who don't have a routine are unlikely to be the ones that are successful as swing traders.

Keep Educating Yourself

As a swing trader, you need to recognize that this is a specialized skill. It's not a hobby, it's a professional activity. In order to succeed at any professional activity, you need to keep up with your education and keep honing and improving your skills. So, you should study swing trading and the financial markets at every opportunity so that over time you are going to become a better trader.

Maintain a Journal

Traders and investors should keep a trading journal. Enter all your activities related to your trading as if it was a diary. You should also keep a section where you keep a record of your trades, including how much you

171

paid to enter the position and how much you got out of it, including losses if they occur. You should also keep a net running total for each month and for the year. It's important to go on actual recorded information in order to know if you are succeeding or failing at trading, rather than going off the hope of a couple of recent wins and fooling yourself by neglecting to remember the losses that have also occurred.

Don't be impulsive

Next to panic when you are facing losses on a trade or greed when you think you can get more and more money, the worst kind of emotion or action that you can take while trading is making impulsive moves. Unfortunately, being impulsive is very common among novice traders.

Impulsive decisions often result from hyper-excitement. A trader might see a trend or hear some news that in their mind makes a trade a "sure thing." Then without doing any kind of analysis, they enter the trade with no planning, and since there was no analysis done, they can quickly find out that the trade goes the wrong way and works against them instead.

Stick to One Trading Technique

Don't try to be a jack of all trades. So, if you want to be a day trader, you should become a day trader. If you want to become a swing trader, then become a swing trader. You shouldn't try being all things at once, even if you hear that others are successful in doing so. Some people can do both styles of trading, while also maintaining long term investments. But most people are not going to find success trying to do everything. Pick one trading style and become an expert at it.

Become an expert on a small number of securities

The market, by its very nature, is volatile. This means that most if not all stocks provide plenty of opportunities to earn money by swing trading. It can help your swing trading if you primarily on a few different stocks. Pick 3-5 to use in order to do your swing trading. Learn the stocks inside and out, so that you know their 52-week highs and lows, and so that you have time to carefully study their charts and look for the right opportunities to enter trades. Having at most five means that you are going to be able to look at the stocks and find good opportunities for swing trading, while not getting overwhelmed. Having at least three ensures that at any given time, you are going to be able to find trades to enter.

Don't be afraid to wait on your trades

As a swing trader, you may be anxious to earn money from your trades, but there is not any rule that says you have to get out of a position before earning the profits that you hope to earn. Unless the stock has crashed down and just isn't going to rebound up to a level where you are able to earn profits, you should be patient and wait long enough for the price to rise to the appropriate pricing level for profits. Unlike day traders, which are high-pressure types that have to act fast, swing trading is a more relaxed and patient trading style. Have the patience to wait overnight, and even weeks if you have to in order to realize your profits.

Don't be afraid to sit on the sidelines

Sometimes, the opportunities to swing trade and earn profits – while still doing the careful analysis – are not going to be there. As a swing trader being anxious is not going to be a helpful characteristic. You are going to want to be able to sit on the sidelines if necessary, waiting for the right trade before you jump into a position. Remember that at the end of the year, your total annual results of wins and losses are what is going to matter. Being constantly in trades is not what matters. So, if you have to wait a few days or even a week to find a solid trade that is likely to be a winner, then be prepared to wait. It is better to wait a few days to get into a winning trade than it is to be impulsive and then have your money tied up in less promising or even losing trades, while you see the good trades pass you by.

CHAPTER 22:

Options Chains

As an investor or even a trader, you should know how to trade options. You should aim to ensure that you have a certain percentage of your investment funds are committed to options trading. Options do not just diversify your portfolio, but they also provide you with immense opportunities of earning large profits with minimal income.

A lot of traders, both small and large, prefer options trading to grow their wealth and benefit from higher profits. This is achievable with relatively small amounts of funds. The profits earned via options are disproportionately large compared to the investments made. One benefit of this type of trading is that you are able to begin small and grow large very fast. With amounts as little as $80, a small retail trader is able to invest in options and see gains very soon.

Option trading is a very versatile process. This opens up a whole new world of opportunities. You could use options basically to trade and earn profits, for leverage and also as insurance or protection against potential losses. All these can be attained conveniently and very quickly.

Caution

Because trading in options is a very powerful process, it is also a very risky one. It is also very dangerous and can get out of hand if not handled carefully. It is crucial that traders and investors understand exactly how to trade options and lots of other details. Getting sufficient knowledge and enough practice is crucial if you are to be successful and consistently profitable.

Reading Options Symbols, Chains, and Tables

Before you can begin trading options, you need to understand the process of buying and selling. You also need to learn how to read tables where options or quotes are printed. There are symbols used when quoting options and tables that consist of a complex array of numbers.

An Introduction to Options Chains

When you want to buy stocks, you have to check prices on a stock quote. A stock quote generally indicates listed stocks and the latest price of each stock. Similarly, if you wish to purchase options, you will check the prices on an options chain.

An options chain is basically a table that lists or outlines the total number of available options based on qualifying stocks. The chain is presented in a number of different ways so learning how to read it is crucial. You should learn how to read an options chain accurately and precisely. This is the very first step if you are to successfully trade in stock options.

Various Types of Options Chains

There are several different options chain formats available. These represent different options information. It is essential to learn a little more about the different formats in common use. This way, you will be conversant with them and be able to use any whenever encountered.

The Basic Call and Put Options Chain

This specific chain is generally the most popular options chain that is used by investors and traders, especially beginners. It is an excellent choice for those seeking to learn more about options. Of all the chains available, the basic call and put options chain is the most basic. It is also the most widely used by investors and traders. On the screen, you will observe information like the bid price, last price, ask price, open interest, volume, and open interest.

Other parameters such as bid price, last price, ask price, volumes, price change from the previous trading day and open interests are displayed for both put and call options. When it comes to trading or investing, this chain is actually the most widely used. It is popular with traders basically because it presents a lot of the information, they consider crucial.

Important information necessary to execute trades is presented in a simple manner that is easy to read and understand. Using this chain, a trader can easily trace and identify available call and put options as well as other parameters affiliated to each option. However, this chain is most suitable for traders interested in simple options trading strategies. There are other chains suitable for more complex strategies.

The Call and Put Options Pricer

The put and call pricer is a chain that presents the necessary data relating to the basic call and put options. It also projects each option with five option Greeks. This way, an investor or trader who needs to use delta neutral options trading strategies and arbitrage strategies. The trader will be able to effectively make exact calculations regarding size and position to take. This particular options chain is more detailed compared to others. All the essential information is presented just like with other chains but also includes details such as the symbols. However, it showcases only call options or put options but never both. This makes it easier for a serious investor or trader to consult and get accurate information.

Looking at a relevant chain, you will easily note that all the five Greek symbols that include Vega, Rho, Theta, Gamma, and Delta are used. They are visible in the call and put options pricer. However, due to challenges in full-screen presentations, options pricers usually present as either put options or call options only.

Options Strategies Chains

This is yet another chain commonly used to present data on available options. This particular chain presents details of options within specific strategies. For instance, you will find a chain that presents the net debit of covered call options at various strike prices complete with relevant information such as assigned and static returns.

Specific options strategies chains are ideal for options traders or investors who prefer standardized options strategies like the covered call or the long straddle. The reason is because these chains drastically reduce the amount of work necessary to work out and calculate the options outlay as well as other specifics that relate to the specific strategy.

Options chains like this one generally present only the essential aspects of a particular options trading strategy across the various expiration dates and strike prices. This way, it is able to easily calculate and work out the net effect of a particular position and plenty of other useful detail. A trader is able to make quick decisions on the spread to choose fast without spending time doing calculations and working out arithmetic.

Call and Put Options Matrix

This particular chain is the least used by investors and traders, especially beginners and retail options traders. This options matrix generally presents only the ask and bid prices for all options listed on the chain but without additional information. This makes it a less useful table especially for beginners, amateurs, and retail traders who basically need a lot more information. However, it is considered by many traders to be the least useful chain out there. This matrix endeavors to present numerous expiration months and strike prices on one page. The aim is often to present as many as is practically possible. Such a chain aims to provide users with as much useful data or information about call and put options as possible.

CHAPTER 23:

Transaction Fees and Slippage

Transaction Costs

Transaction costs, also called transaction fees, are the charges related to the execution of a trade or the expression of an intention to maintain a position. As such, in options, the exchange gees, brokerage commissions and the Securities and Exchange Commission (SEC) fees count as the transaction costs.

Typically, brokerage commission is paid on a per-contract basis, and it pays for the services the trading platform renders like customer service and the execution of orders. The SEC fees are destined to take care of regulatory functions by the governing body. The exchange fees are a special fee to compensate markets for running a reliable and robust marketplace. If the investor wants to use his margin interest to complete a transaction, he must pay some margin interest. This makes margin interest the money that is charged for borrowing money from the brokerage.

Before you go ahead placing your order, ensure that you understand, and account for all the transaction costs that have to do with attaining and maintaining the position you have taken. The transaction cots affect much more besides the premiums you have paid or have received after the purchase or the sale of an option. Therefore, if you want to break even every time, ensure that you consider all variables involved in the trade, including the premium you paid at first, the option contract's strike price, and the transaction costs the brokerage firm charges.

Slippage

Slippage can also happen after a large order has been executed, although there is usually not enough volume at the time, and at that price, to maintain the current ask and bid spreads.

The change in price during a slippage is either negative or positive because it all depends on the direction the price has taken. It matters whether you are going short or long and whether you are closing or opening a position. As such, a slippage is any deviation from your trade strategy. Whichever direction the deviation heads, the slippage lowers the trader's confidence in the strategy's intended outcome.

If slippage is not well modeled, even a theoretically sound strategy could yield negative returns. If a seemingly positive winning strategy produces negative results, it means that the trader is yet to attain the best execution, and he may need to perform some auditing to determine the best execution policy. As such, proactively managing the slippage is likely to produce greater confidence in the overall trading strategy.

An example of slippage would be if you were closing a long position with the intended sale order placed at $100.20. If the order is executed at $100.15, you get a negative $0.05 slip. If the same order is completed at $100.25, it will have gotten a $0.05 positive slip.

If the slippage affects your positions, you still might be lucky to find some brokers who would be willing to fill your orders, but they can only do so at the worse price. However, the best trading platforms' execution practices ensure that once the price has shifted outside of your tolerance level, any time between when you placed your order and the time of execution, the order will be rejected. Their reason for doing this is to protect you from the adverse effects of slippage as you open and close your position. However, if the situation changes and the price move to a better position, your brokerage would fill your order at the better, more favorable price.

Other ways to protect yourself from the effects of slippage is to install limits or some stop losses on your active positions. The limits help to avoid slippage as you enter or close your position because a limit order only fills at the price you have stipulated prior. On the other hand, the stop loss closes out your trade immediately; your asset's price hits the particular level you had specified. If the asset price is triggered, you are required to pay a premium.

When Does A Slippage Occur?

We have established that slippage occurs when there is high market volatility or low market liquidity. In a low liquidity market, the market participants are often very few, and this means that there are not many traders on the other end of a trade. In this case, it takes much longer to execute a trade because the seller often has to wait for a long time to get a buyer. In the course of the delay, asset prices change, and in a volatile market, this could happen in a split second; sometimes, in the few seconds, a trader will take to fill his order.

Slippages are most prevalent around the time when major news events are happening, such as when a major bank is announcing changes regarding its monetary policies or its interest rates. A major company announcing significant changes, such as when it presents its earnings reports or announces changes in its leadership, often produces the same result. Events like these increase market volatilities and increase the possibility of experiencing a slippage.

Unfortunately, many of these significant events, like a company announcing a change in its leadership, are not often predictable. However, others like the reading of company financial reports, announcements by the central bank on different monetary policies, and major meetings like those of the Federal Reserve are scheduled, and traders can speculate what is to be talked about in those meetings. These predictions are not always right.

Other Strategies to Help Avoid Slippage

There are three other smart ways to minimize slippage and its effects on your trading.

Set up Some Limit Orders and Guaranteed Stops to Your Order Positions

Guaranteed stops, unlike other kinds of stops, are not subject to slippage, and will, therefore, ensure that your trade closes at the exact point you have set. This makes the guaranteed stops the ultimate way to manage risks when a market is moving against you. Keep in mind, however, that a guaranteed stop, unlike other stops, will require that you pay a premium once it is triggered.

Limit orders are also useful for mitigating risks that come with slippage as you enter a trade, and when you want to make a profit from a winning trade. When you have a limit order, your order will only be occupied at your predetermined price, even if the limit order is triggered.

Limit Your Trading Activity to Markets with High Liquidity and Low Volatility

If you keep to markets with low volatility and high liquidity, you will have avoided the primary causes of slippage: high volatility and low liquidity. Low volatility means that the price will not be changing too quickly, while a high liquidity market is one where there are many active participants on either side of the trades.

In the same way, you can also reduce the possibility of slippage if you limit your trading to the hours when there is the highest market activity because that is when the market is liquid. At this time, your orders stand a higher chance of being executed at your requested price, unlike when the market is less liquid.

The time when the US market is most liquid is when exchanges like the New York Stock Exchange and the NASDAQ are open. At this time, the trading volume is very high. The same is the case for the forex market because even though the market runs 24 hours every day, the best time to trade is when the London Stock Exchange is open.

If you ignore this rule and decide to hold positions when the markets are closed, such as during the weekend or at night, you are likely to suffer slippage. Slippage happens when the market reopens, and the prices have changed. The news, events of the night or morning, and other announcements will have had an effect on the financial market.

See How Your Broker Treats Slippage

If, when opening or closing a position, the price moves against you, some brokers might still execute your orders. However, this is not the proper thing to do because your broker should never fill your orders at a worse level than the one you have requested because it might be rejected.

A good broker sets a tolerance level on either side of your predetermined closing price, and if the market remains within this range at the time when the broker receives your order, your trade will be executed as the level you have requested. However, if the price steps out of this range, the brokerage does one of two things.

If the market shifts and the price is better, the broker will ensure your order closes at that better price so you can enjoy some additional profit. If, on the other hand, the market moves against you, beyond the brokerage's tolerance, the brokers ought to reject that order then ask you to resubmit your order it at the current level.

CHAPTER 24:

How to Maximize Profits with Options

N ow it is time to move on to some of the steps that you can take in order to maximize your profits with the help of options. Options are a great way to earn a profit because they allow you a way to reduce your exposure and the amount of risk that you take on, while increasing the amount of profits that you could potentially make. some of the tips that you can use to help maximize your profits while options trading includes:

Tip 1: You can profit no matter the market situation

One of the first things that you will notice when you are working in the options market is that you can actually benefit from any situation in the market when you work with options. Most of the strategies that work with this investment vehicle are carried out by combining the different option positions, and sometimes they will even use the underlying position of the stock. Basically, you can use either different trading strategies, or work with a few together, to profit no matter what market situation is going on.

When you enter into the market with options, you always stand to make a huge amount of profits, while still keeping your risk to a minimum. Ordinary stock trading isn't as reliable, and it comes with a lot more risk. The most crucial aspects of options trading are to know when you should enter a trade and how you should exit it. Knowing how and when to exit will ensure that you keep any losses to a minimum and that you can increase your profits as much as possible.

You will find that options strategies are considered one of the most versatile when it comes to the financial market. They are going to provide investors and traders alike with a lot of profit-making opportunities, and there is a limited amount of risk and exposure present. This is one of the main reasons that a lot of investors like to take some time and invest in options instead of the other asset choices.

Since you are able to profit no matter what the market situation is doing, this gives you a lot of freedom when working with options. But it also means that you may have to learn a lot more strategies than usual. You should learn at least a few strategies for a rising market, for a stagnant market, and for a downturn market. This will ensure that you are ready to go no matter which way the market is heading.

While the ability to make a profit in any kind of market is a great thing and can open up many new opportunities to make money compared to just investing in the stock market, it does make things a bit trickier to work with. You have to understand where the market is going, you have to know which strategies work for the different market directions, and you have to be ready to switch back and forth depending on how the market is doing.

Tip 2: Take advantage of the volatility of options to make a profit

Options have some similarities to stocks, but they are a bit different. And one place you will notice these differences is with the time limit. Stocks can be held for as short of a time period, or as long of a time period, as you want, but options have an expiration date. This means that the time you get to do the trade is going to be limited. And as a trader, missing this window is going to be a costly mistake, one that you need to avoid if at all possible. If this chance is missed, then it may be a very long time before you see it again.

This is why it is never a good idea to work with a long-term strategy when you are trying to trade with options. Strategies, such as working with the average down, are seen as bad choices for options trading because you simply don't get the right time frame to see them happen. Also, make sure that you are careful about margin requirements. Depending on what these are, they could have a big impact on the requirements for the amount of funds you are able to invest.

There are also times when multiple factors may affect a favorable price. For instance, the price of the asset you choose may go up, which is usually seen as a good thing. But it is possible that any of the accruing benefits could be eroded due to other factors, such as volatility, time decay, and dividend payment. These constraints mean that you need to learn how to follow some of the different strategies for profit-taking.

Tip 3: Always set a profit taking stop loss

The next tip that you should follow is to set up a profit taking stop loss. You can set up a stop loss at about five percent. This means that you want it to reach a target price of $100 if the trailing target is going to be $95. If the upward trend does continue and the price gets to $120, then the trailing target, assuming the 5 percent from before, is going to become $114. And it would keep going up from there, with the amount of profit that you wish to make in the process.

Now, let's say that the price is going to start to fall. When this happens, you will need to exit and then collect the profits at this level, or the trailing target that you set. This ensures that you get to enjoy some protection as the price increases, and then you will exit the trade as soon as the price starts to turn around. The thing that you need to remember here is that the stop loss levels should never be too high or too low. If they are too small, you will be kicked out of the market too soon in most cases. But if they are too large, they will make it impossible to enjoy profit taking.

Tip 4: Sell covered call options against long positions

Selling options Is an income generating process that is pretty lucrative. Depending on the amount of risk that you take and what kinds of trades you decide to do, you could easily take home more than two percent in returns each month. However, this is not the only method you can use in order to make it rich on the market. You can also go with something that is known as a naked put and sell these. This is similar in a way to selling stocks or shares that you don't actually own.

When you go through the process of selling a naked put options, you will be able to free up some of your time to do more. Stock trading allows you to have an opportunity to sell stocks of shares that you don't already own, and then you can earn a profit. This will free up your capital, allowing you to invest it or trade with it indefinitely.

To make this method work, it is best if you work with stocks that you already understand well, or those that you wouldn't mind actually owning. This way, you know when there are any major changes to the stock, and you can make some changes to the way you invest before the market turns and harms your profits. There is still a level of hedging that is associated with this options trading method, so you must always be on the lookout for that.

Tip 5: Pick the right strategy

And often the one that you pick will lead you to finding the right options to sell. Some of the options trading strategies are going to work in a downturn, some are going to work the best in an upturn, and some do well when the market is more stagnant. When you pick out a strategy, you will then be able to choose the options that fit in with that strategy the best.

With that said, there are a few guidelines that you can learn to follow when it is time to purchase an option for trading. Following these guidelines will make it easier for you to identify the options that you should choose in order to make a good profit. Some of the guidelines include:

Determine whether the market is bullish or bearish. Also, make sure that you determine whether you are really strongly bullish, or just mildly bullish. This can make a difference in how the market is doing and which assets you would like to work with.

Think about how volatile the market is right now and how it could affect your strategy with options trading. Also, you can think about the status of the market at the time. Is the market currently calm or is there a lot of volatility that shows up? If it is not very high, then you should be able to buy the call options based on the underlying stock, and these are usually seen as relatively inexpensive.

Consider the strike price and the expiration date of any options you want to trade in. If you only have a few shares at this time, then this may make it the best time to purchase more of the stock or asset.

Your overall goal of working with the options trading market is to make as much profit as possible. No one goes into the market, or any kind of investment, with the idea that they want to lose money. But if you follow some of the tips above, you will be able to maximize your profits and see some great results.

195

CHAPTER 25:

Choose the Right Market

U nderstanding the market conditions is crucial as you begin your journey towards becoming a seasoned swing trader.

Patience is crucial in this kind of trading. You will be waiting out for the best prevailing conditions so that you will then move in to close and make profits within a limited period. As such, it then becomes critical that you understand the market conditions that affect the prices of trading. This understanding helps you not just in knowing whether you will make a profit or not, but also in speculating, a significant factor in the trading sector.

To understand market conditions, then, is to strategize on how you will go about your trading venture. In trading, the market moves in what traders call waves, and these waves can be either impulsive or corrective. Sudden surges usually go with the trend, while corrective waves run counter to this, acting to correct the impulse waves. Understanding this, then becomes key in how you will trade at a given moment.

Trendlines

Trendlines are critical components of the trading market. In swing trading, they are essential, as you will see to close and make profits within a specified set of times.

This move of identifying and confirming trends is called moving average. Further, you will need to understand a step called the simple moving average (SMA). Here, you will take all the closing prices for a select number of days then add them up. Then, you will receive the total you get and divide it by itself. The answer is the average price of the security exchange.

When you do this over several different select days, it gives an idea of what is happening in the market. This idea will help you understand whether putting in your money on a given trend is worth it.

When you take the time to understand the market, then, when you do your mathematics, the general trend of the market price when you put it in a graph will provide you with how the market is or has been performing through the selected number of days. If the general movement of the chart points upwards, then it shows you that the prices of security are going up. If it looks downwards over the select period, then the prices are going down, Trend up and trend down.

To further smoothen how the SMA performs, you can enhance it through the exponential moving average (EMA). The EMA provides trends that give details of more recent data, unlike the SMA, which is broader. To determine the current prices, many traders will go with the EMA as it readily lends itself to helping you calculate the more recent rates in the market.

197

A(n) then stands for the price of the asset at a given period while (n) represents the period and the total number of periods.

As we can see, then, to understand how the market goes, then it is vital that you get to know how trends will affect how you trade and whether you will make a profit or not.

To make money off from trend trading, though, you will need to get in early then hold your place until the trend reverses. What this then means is that you will need to make a proper assessment that the prices will keep moving in the direction that you want and will not change along the way.

Because of this, the risks of trading off the trend is higher, and thus, you will need to be rigorous in your risk assessment.

However, the higher risk of trend trade means then that you are also likely to make huge profits when it does go right. When you make your move at just the right time, and hold out, you will then reap significantly from it.

Range

In stock trading, the range is the difference between the buying price and the selling price at the highs and lows of the stock market.

Some traders will often attempt to trade within ranges, rather than through following trends, in what is known as range trading. Unlike the trend trader, the range trader does not give much emphasis on the direction of the graph. Their thinking is that, no matter how far the currency falls or rises, since it will most often revert to its natural point, they then place their money on this. So, they make their money by capitalizing on this undulating movement of the prices over and over again.

As we see, this requires a very different type of management from the trend and will need you to be willing to be wrong at the start of the trade. Here, you do not need to assess the market movement. This assessment then allows you to build on the trading position that you got in.

Still, you need to identify the range in your assessment. You will need to identify the points at which the currency has fallen into or risen into at least twice, before recovering. The two locations do not need to be identical but close to each other and similar.

Therefore, based on this, range trading is one that will generate profits for you, but as with any investment, it comes with its risks, and you will need to be on the lookout.

When you do not intend on trading on the range, you will still need to understand it as it will guide you in making the calculations that come with placing your bet on the stocks. The scale will also allow you to know which currencies you would want to trade-in. Stronger currency pairs often will have shorter ranges, but because of their stability, they will then be close to a guarantee that you will make your profits. They also

199

trade frequently, which then means that you will be able to make cumulative profits from the small margins that the deal offers.

Relative Strength Index

RSI, as many traders call it, is a central unit of assessment in the stock market.

The RSI will be what will help you gain entry into the market. So, what is the relative strength index?

The RSI is an indicator that will help you with looking into the short signals under the presumption that the prices have drastically been oscillating that the market ends up overbought or oversold.

The RSI will be a great companion for you when you begin to make your entry into the trading. Because you will need to understand how the market moves, the RSI then provides you will have an opportunity to look into the data and determine how the market is moving.

The RSI, as with many indicators in the trade business, will provide you with details on what trade opportunities are great for you.

However, many trading experts generally agree that you will be better off using the RSI, among other trading technical tools. To know that trade will yield the returns you want, you will need all these indicators to all give you the same or similar data. This result is because, through analyzing the market from different angles, one can then make their choice based on the consistent feed that they receive from the various indicators.

So, this will mean that aside from the RSI, you will also need candlesticks and moving averages, as well as the volumes traded to tell you the whole story. The information does not necessarily have to be within the same day. However, they need to be consistent enough so that they are within the same time frame, such as in a span of one or two, or at most, three days.

However, when you make this trade, understand that trading does not have a complete guarantee that you will make the profits that you so wish to make. As one trader put it 'there isn't a magic bullet.' You will need to take the risk without having to hold out for too long. As such, these technical analysis tools should only be a guide to you. You will need to put your money into the trade at the end of the day, with all the risks hanging up over your head. As such, the analysis is only part of the deal. You will need to put your hands down and get down to business.

Understand Group of Stock

Group of stocks is the select number of commodities that you keep an eye on as they should be the ones that you have selected to trade. This group of stock will include currencies, gold, and oil, among many others.

Understanding the group of stock will need you always to keep your eyes off the ground, following through the news so that you are well aware of the small changes within. In trading, small changes will often have significant changes, and you will need to continually be mindful so that you do not get checked out and find yourself at a disadvantage.

The changes let you understand the portfolio package and the number of stocks within the box, as well as give you indicators on the charts. Trading will need you to have a clear plan, with it being that when you move in, you will need to have a target and a limit. Then you will need to have the last point of loss you will take before you opt-out of the deal.

When you take the time to understand it, you will then stop yourself from impulse buying, which, while it can work out for you sometimes, the fact that it will take you off your plans means that it will often become less of trading and more of gambling.

CHAPTER 26:

Start with the Simulator

Investing in the stock market, as the experts point out, requires substantial knowledge and experience to control the risk and make the appropriate decisions at the right time. That is why a virtual stock market simulator can become a fundamental tool to start trading with securities eliminating the dangers one can't afford much with one's hard-earned capital.

These simulators generally offer very advanced interfaces, a virtual economic fund to invest, and real-time information. That is to say; they have all the tools and functions necessary to learn how to invest in an online stock market as if we were in the stock market itself.

Many of these computer programs belong to banks and brokers specialized in the stock market or markets such as Forex (such as Plus500). These applications, from our point of view, are more complete than the simple stock market games that we have found in the market for decades or than the apps that have overwhelmingly increased in recent years.

We are going to analyze five exciting simulators for beginners, so that you can get valuable experience in a virtual stock exchange system before giving way to the real world. Most offer free demo accounts, although in some cases, we can find companies that request a small payment in exchange for using their platform. A small expense that is worth taking on, and that can save us many dislikes in the future.

Why Use A Bag Simulator?

Investing in the stock market is not especially difficult, but it is essential to have good knowledge to avoid greater evils. If you want to achieve high profitability, you have to take risks, but doing it blindly can be a real disaster for our pocket. It can be suicidal, financially speaking.

That is why it is essential to train previously in everything related to the markets and their operation. For this, you can go to the editorial fund of the National Commission of the Stock Market or the Madrid Stock Exchange, where we can find practical guides and handy tips for beginners and more advanced investors.

Having the advice of an expert is also a guarantee, but if you prefer to take the road alone, we recommend that you settle the bases well before playing with real money. The risk, as we have repeated, is high if it is operated without the necessary knowledge. The stock market is not a lottery that can make you rich by investing a few euros, so you should know all the mechanisms of the market entirely to understand where and when to put your money.

In this learning process, a good stock market simulator plays an essential role. With these tools, you can play with fictitious money, see how your decisions affect your income statement, and, most importantly, create solid pillars to leap to the real world of investments.

Another advantage is that the companies that offer these simulators allow you to directly operate with real money from the same or similar platform, so you will already be familiar with the interface. In many cases, it is only necessary to convert your demo account into a real account and make an income, without changing the program.

Pay for a bag simulator?

Many people are wondering what the best free bag simulator for beginners is. It is true that in the market, we can find compelling tools that do not require the payment of any amount.

Creating a CFD bag simulator that offers guarantees entails a considerable programming expense and high operating costs. That is why some companies ask for a small subscription in exchange for their use that does not usually reach 10 euros per month. A minimum amount for a tool that tells you how to learn to invest in the stock market from home and that allows you to practice with all the guarantees; it's worth it by any standards, of course.

Also, it is widespread that with that small fee, the user has access to manuals, tutorials, webinars, and other teaching materials to support the practical part with theoretical foundations. Investing in the stock market in the short term is not recommended, so all this material can be of high relevance to fix concepts.

The Best Bag Simulators

Once this preamble has been completed, we will analyze five of the most exciting simulators in the market. All are backed by companies with ample experience in the sector (they are banks or brokers) and are well above in quality and performance of simple stock games (we do not recommend using these games as part of your training). This listing is sorted alphabetically.

Active Trade

This real-time stock market simulator offers users an account with 100,000 virtual euros so they can practice without fear of losing their money. It has personalized support and, most importantly, with courses and trading programs taught by professional traders.

With this tool, you can create your strategy, control your investments, find the companies that best fit your profile, and get detailed information on more than 18,400 shares. Essential functions to create your profile as an investor and locate those opportunities that you can take advantage of in the real world.

IG Spain

The demo account of this stock market simulator allows you to invest in an online stock market in a risk-free environment. This free account has a virtual fund of

20,000 euros and offers graphics and prices in real-time. Also, you can check from your mobile or tablet to continue operating anywhere, even if you don't have a computer. The interface can be customized to suit your tastes and your style.

This demo account, however, does not offer all the functionality of the real platform. The most notable differences are the following:

Transactions made through the demo account are not subject to slippage, interest or dividend adjustments, or price movements out of the negotiation.

Transactions can be rejected if you do not have enough funds to open them, but they will not be denied due to size or price issues.

The graphics packages have not cost.

The positions will not be closed if you do not have enough funds to cover the margin or current losses, something that does happen in a real account.

Orey iTrade

Another easy-to-use bag simulator is that of Orey iTrade. With this tool, you will learn to invest in both the Spanish selective, that is, in the IBEX 35, as in other critical global exchanges. All online and free, since you can try it without cost and obligation.

Through its interface, you can access stock quotes in real-time and different analyses, comparative, and graphical tools. The account begins with a virtual fund of 100,000 euros to start investing.

Société Générale

This trading simulator seems to us one of the most interesting since it will allow you to delve into the world of warrants, something that is not available in most of the free tools. The simulator of this French bank makes available to its users 10,000 fictitious euros to negotiate on the listed products of Société Générale and test their investment strategy without risk.

To start operating, you must register on the website www.sgbolsa.es. Registration is free. Also, the entity usually raffles gifts such as mobile phones or tablets among its new users, one more argument to try the Market Simulator, as they call it.

To use the system, follow these steps:

Register on the website www.Warrants.com.

Connect to the website www.Warrants.com or the simulator using the e-mail and the registration password.

Access the simulator from the Tools menu of the website www.Warrants.com.

Tradertwit

The Tradertwit simulator catches our attention since it has enormous educational value. It is not free (although it is cheap), but instead offers training and a compelling platform. They have a lot of news from the sector, an exciting collaborative platform, and thousands of interactive analyses.

We like what they call "the challenge." It is something like a 50-level training program that puts users in challenges to move from level to level. In each of them, you have to follow instructions, such as the maximum lever that can be used or the maximum loss streak. There are also objectives to be achieved.

Based on these criteria, the user can carry out operations of buying and selling currencies, indices, or raw materials — an excellent way to learn while having fun and competing against other users in the community. Also, the best usually takes real prizes.

CHAPTER 27:

A Strategy for Passive Income in 7 Days

As promised, this book is meant to help you increase your passive income in just 7 days. Since you are day trading, you should be able to earn profits every single day from your trades. With that being said, you are going to want to be earning above your investment income so you can have profits that you actually feel comfortable cashing out with! To help you get started with the best strategy for you to win with, I have outlined three ways that you can start making massive profits in just 7 days.

If you follow this exact blueprint, you will be making profits quickly, allowing you to completely change the scope of your finances both now and in the future. After you have made your profits within 7 days' time, you can go ahead and "rinse and repeat" by applying this same method over and over again, enabling you to continue earning and increasing profits from your trades.

Choosing Your Day to Day Strategy

The first seven days of trading are crucial, but so is every single day after that. For that reason, we are going to look at the first seven days and then every day following as two separate things. The first seven days will help you build your foundation whereas every day afterward will help you maintain that foundation and continue earning a strong profit.

For the first seven days of your trading, you need to decide what you are going to do that is going to help you earn the most profits possible. Since you are likely to brand new to day trading options, I suggest starting out fairly modestly to ensure that you do not get too overwhelmed. If you overwhelm yourself early on it could make trading harder in the future.

I suggest starting in the simplest way possible by using the following strategy:

On day one, complete one trade

On day two, complete two trades

On day three, complete two trades

On day four, complete three trades

On day five, complete three trades

On day six, complete four trades

On day seven, complete four trades

At this point, you can either stay with completing four separate trades (or trade strategies) every single day, or you can further increase the number that you manage until you are reaching your desired profits. Make sure that you never exceed a number that you can reasonably manage to avoid overwhelming

213

yourself and possibly tanking several trades due to confusion and overwhelm.

When you have reached your chosen number of daily trades, stay there and consider that to be your daily strategy. Ideally, you should never exceed this number of trades on any given day so that you can earn your profits while still staying level-headed and calm enough to manage them all. Make sure that you factor your everyday routine for other areas of your life into how many trades you take on, as you are not going to want to overload your schedule. If you are doing this for passive income, you will not want to spend every minute that the stock market is open glued to your computer as a professional day trader would.

Building Your Own Routine

When you start out trading, I strongly advise you to start out by building your own routine right from day one. Take the time to decide what time you like to check in on the markets, when you are going to start your watchlist and technical analysis, and how you are generally going to engage in trading.

If you need to set alarms each morning to alert you throughout the day, make that a part of your routine. If you like to sit down with a cup of coffee and your tablet so you can check in on the market each morning, make that a part of your routine. If you like to check in on your lunch break and your afternoon break, make that a part of your routine.

Creating a routine in trading is less about having a frivolous schedule to follow and more about instilling strong habits into your trade strategy from the very beginning so that you always make the best moves possible. This way, you can feel confident that you will not miss out on the best positions, mismanage your trades, or forget about your trades and have them canceled at the end of the trading day. As a result, you will be able to feel more confident in your trading and trade management strategies while also continually improving your strategies as you go.

The 30% Rule

Lastly, I present to you the 30% rule. The 30% rule has less to do with your bottom line and actual trade strategy and more to do with your money management strategy. When it comes to trading as a way to earn any form of income, even a passive income, you want to make sure that you are never cashing out on more profits than you can reasonably handle. The idea with trading is that you will create profits that increase the amount of investment capital over time, meaning that you can afford to make larger investments and therefore earn larger profits from your trades. With that being said, you do want to make sure that you are cashing out on some of your capital to ensure that you are always earning an income from this strategy which makes it worthwhile. The 30% rule states that you never take more than 30% of the profits that you earn from each trade out of your trading account. So, if you invest $50 into a trade and earn $150 from it, your profit is $100.

Conclusion

First of all, we would point out that the whole guide was written without relying on any kind of fees. As we already mentioned, fees vary, and every brokerage house has its own rules about it.

·   Trading options have significant risks. If you are absolutely inexperienced with trading, we would recommend talking with a financial advisor before making any decision.

·   Always keep in mind that every investment has its own risk and reward rating which means that if the risk is high, the reward will be high too.

·   Expiration date of American style options and European style options (the most commonly used ones) is always the third Saturday in the month for American and the last Friday before the third Saturday for European options.

·   Phrase ''in the money'' describes that the option has a value higher than the strike price for call options and lower than the strike price for put options at the time of their expiration.

·   The most common minimal bid for option sharing is one nickel or 5 dollars per contract. However, some more liquid contracts allow minimal bid to be one dollar per contract.

- 100 shares of the certain stock are actually 1 option contract

- If you pay 1 dollar for an option your premium for that option whether you buy or sell it is 1 dollar per share, which means that the option premium is 100 dollars per contract

- All of the examples in this guide assume that every option order ever mentioned was filled successfully.

- Whenever you want to open a new position you will have to sell or buy on the market to ''open''. The same principle applies if you wish to close your position. You sell or buy to ''close''.

- Phrase Open Interest represents the number of option contracts that are opened at the moment. Logically- more opened contracts mean a bigger number and closed contracts mean a smaller number.

- Volume of the options is the number of contracts that are traded in one single day.

Be careful when signing the contracts; make sure you read all of the trading options.

So here we are at the end of this guidebook on trading options. They can be extremely profitable but learning to trade them well takes time. You can choose to use indicators to determine your entry points, and I'm all for this approach at first but remember that over the long term, you're better served learning the basics of order flow and using that.

There is no shortage of options strategies you can use to dramatically limit your risk and depending on the volatility levels, you can deploy separate strategies to achieve the same ends. Contrast this with a directional trading strategy where you have just one method of entry, which is to either go short or go long, and only one way of managing risk, which is to use a stop loss.

Spread or market neutral trading puts you in the position of not having to care about what the market does. In addition, it brings another dimension of the market into focus, which is volatility. Volatility is the greatest thing for your gains and options allow you to take full advantage of this, no matter what the volatility situation currently is.

Options can be a bit hard to get your head around at first since so many of us are used to looking at the market as a thing that goes up or down. Options bring a sideways and a different vertical element to it via spreads and volatility estimates. More advanced options strategies take full advantage of volatility and are more math-focused, so if this interests you, you should go for them.

That being said, do not assume the complexity means more gains. The strategies shown here are quite simple, and they will make you money thanks to the way options are structured. They bring you the advantage of leverage without having to borrow a single cent.

You can choose to borrow, of course, but you need to do this only if it is in line with your risk management math. Risk management is what will make or break your results and at the center of quantitative risk management is your risk per trade. Keep this consistent and line up your success rate and reward to risk ratios, and you'll make money as a mathematical certainty.

Qualitative risk management requires you to adopt the right mindset with regards to trading, and it is crucial for you to adopt this as quickly as possible. Remember that the implications of your risk math mean that you need not be concerned with the outcome of a single trade. Instead, seek to maximize your gains over the long term.

The learning curve might get steep at times, but given the rewards on offer, this is a small price to pay. Keep hammering away at your skills, and soon you'll find yourself trading options profitably, and everything will be worth it. How much can you expect to make trading options?

Well, I previously said that I'm not keen on putting numbers to this sort of thing. Generally, a good options trade can expect around 50-80% returns on their capital. As you grow in size, this return amount will decrease naturally. However, to start off with these are beyond excellent returns.

Always make sure you're well capitalized since this is the downfall of many traders. You need to be patient with the process. A lot of people rush headfirst into the market without adequate capitalization or learning and soon find that the markets are far tougher than they

thought. So always ensure the mental stress you place yourself in is low and that you're never in a position where you 'have' to make money trading.

I wish you the best of luck in all of your trading efforts. The key to success is to simply never give up and to be resilient. Reduce the stress on yourself, and you'll be fine. Here's wishing you all the success in your options trading journey!

CPSIA information can be obtained
at www.ICGtesting.com
Printed in the USA
BVHW021410091222
653826BV00015B/9